Our Hearts Wait

The Walter Brueggemann Library

Davis Hankins, *Editor*

Other books in this series:

Deliver Us: Salvation and the Liberating God of the Bible

Our Hearts Wait

Worshiping through Praise and Lament in the Psalms

Walter Brueggemann

WESTMINSTER
JOHN KNOX PRESS
LOUISVILLE · KENTUCKY

First edition
Published by Westminster John Knox Press
Louisville, Kentucky

22 23 24 25 26 27 28 29 30 31—10 9 8 7 6 5 4 3 2 1

Book design by Sharon Adams
Cover design by designpointinc.com

Library of Congress Cataloging-in-Publication Data

Names: Brueggemann, Walter, author.
Title: Our hearts wait : worshiping through praise and lament in the Psalms
  / Walter Brueggemann.
Description: First edition. | Louisville , Kentucky: Westminster John Knox
  Press, 2022. | Series: The Walter Brueggemann Library ; volume 2 |
  Summary: "Drawn from numerous publications in recent decades, this
  volume traces how the language of longing and gratitude in the Psalms
  offers a template for liturgies that shape not only our collective
  worship and communities, but also the worlds they create and sustain"--
  Provided by publisher.
Identifiers: LCCN 2022033445 (print) | LCCN 2022033446 (ebook) | ISBN
  9780664265892 (paperback) | ISBN 9781646982851 (ebook)
Subjects: LCSH: Bible. Psalms--Criticism, interpretation, etc. | Laments in
  the Bible. | Worship.
Classification: LCC BS1430.52 .B784 2022 (print) | LCC BS1430.52 (ebook)
  | DDC 223/.206--dc23/eng/20220912
LC record available at https://lccn.loc.gov/2022033445
LC ebook record available at https://lccn.loc.gov/2022033446

To Kathleen M. O'Connor, Christine Roy Yoder, William P. Brown,
and Brennan W. Breed, for sustaining vibrant study of
Old Testament traditions at Columbia Theological Seminary

Contents

Part Four: Hope and Thanksgiving

Series Preface

I have been very pleased that David Dobson and his staff at Westminster John Knox Press have proposed this extended series of republications of my work. Indeed, I know of no old person who is not pleased to be taken seriously in old age! My first thought, in learning of this proposed series, is that my life and my work have been providentially fortunate in having good companions all along the way who have both supported me and for the most part kept me honest in my work. I have been blessed by the best teachers, who have prepared me to think both critically and generatively. I have been fortunate to be accompanied by good colleagues, both academic and pastoral, who have engaged my work. And I have been gifted to have uncommonly able students, some of whom continue to instruct me in the high art of Old Testament study.

The long years of my work that will be represented in this series reflect my slow process of finding my own voice, of sorting out accents and emphases, and of centering my work on recurring themes that I have judged to merit continuing attention. The result of that slow process is that over time my work is marked by repetition and reiteration, as well as contradiction, change of mind, and ambiguity, all of which belongs to seeing my work as an organic whole as I have been given courage and insight. In the end I have settled on recurring themes (reflected in the organization of this series) that I hope I have continued to treat with imagination, so that my return to them is not simply reiteration but is critically generative of new perspective and possibility.

In retrospect I can identify two learnings from the philosopher and hermeneut Paul Ricoeur that illumine my work. Ricoeur has given me names for what I have been doing, even though I was at work on such matters before I acquired Ricoeur's terminology. First, in his book *Freud and Philosophy* (1965), Ricoeur identifies two moves that are essential for interpretation. On the one hand there is "suspicion." By this term Ricoeur means critical skepticism. In biblical study "suspicion" has taken the form of historical criticism in which the interpreter doubts the "fictive" location and function of the text and hypothesizes about the "real, historical" location and function of the text. On the other hand there is "retrieval," by which Ricoeur means the capacity to reclaim what is true in the text after due "suspicion." My own work has included measures of "suspicion" because a grounding in historical criticism has been indispensable for responsible interpretation. My work, however, is very much and increasingly tilted toward "retrieval," the recovery of what is theologically urgent in the text. My own location in a liberal-progressive trajectory of interpretation has led me to an awareness that liberal-progressives are tempted to discard "the baby" along with "the bath." For that reason my work has been to recover and reclaim, I hope in generative imaginative ways, the claims of biblical faith.

Second and closely related, Ricoeur has often worked with a grid of "precritical/critical/postcritical" interpretation. My own schooling and that of my companions has been in a critical tradition; that enterprise by itself, however, has left the church with little to preach, teach, or trust. For that reason my work has become increasingly postcritical, that is, with a "second naiveté" a readiness to engage in serious ways the claims of the text. I have done so in a conviction that the alternative metanarratives available to us are inadequate and the core claims of the Bible are more adequate for a life of responsible well-being. Both liberal-progressive Christians and fundamentalist Christians are tempted and seduced by alternative narratives that are elementally inimical to the claims of the Bible; for that reason the work of a generative exposition of biblical claims seems to me urgent. Thus I anticipate that this series may be a continuing invitation to the ongoing urgent work of exposition that both makes clear the singular claims of the Bible and exposes the inadequacy of competing narratives that, from a biblical perspective, amount to idolatry. It is my hope that such continuing work will not only give preachers something substantive to preach and give teachers something substantive to teach, but will invite the church to embrace the biblical claims that it can "trust and obey."

My work has been consistently in response to the several unfolding crises facing our society and, more particularly, the crises faced by the church. Strong market forces and ideological passions that occupy center stage among us sore tempt the church to skew its tradition, to compromise its gospel claim, and to want to be "like the nations" (see 1 Sam. 8:5, 20), that is, without the embarrassment of gospel disjunction. Consequently I have concluded, over time, that our interpretive work must be more radical in its awareness that the claims of faith increasingly contradict the dominant ideologies of our time. That increasing awareness of contradiction is ill-served by progressive-liberal accommodation to capitalist interests and, conversely, it is ill-served by the packaged reductions of reactionary conservatism. The work we have now to do is more complex and more demanding than either progressive-liberal or reactionary-conservative offers. Thus our work is to continue to probe this normative tradition that is entrusted to us that is elusive in its articulation and that hosts a Holy Agent who runs beyond our explanatory categories in irascible freedom and in bottomless fidelity.

I am grateful to the folk at Westminster John Knox and to a host of colleagues who continue to engage my work. I am profoundly grateful to Davis Hankins, on the one hand, for his willingness to do the arduous work of editing this series. On the other hand I am grateful to Davis for being my conversation partner over time in ways that have evoked some of my better work and that have fueled my imagination in fresh directions. I dare anticipate that this coming series of republication will, in generative ways beyond my ken, continue to engage a rising generation of interpreters in bold, courageous, and glad obedience.

Walter Brueggemann

Editor's Introduction

I began theological education just as Walter Brueggemann was scheduled to retire at Columbia Theological Seminary. I knew very little about the academic study of religion, probably even less about the state of biblical scholarship at the turn of the twenty-first century, yet somehow I knew enough to take every possible course with Dr. Brueggemann. After retiring, Walter continued to teach a course periodically and work from his study on campus—and he always insisted that it and any pastor's work space be called a "study" rather than an "office"! But before he retired, during his last and my first year at Columbia, I took six different courses in biblical studies, including three with Walter. In my memory, I spent that academic year much like St. Thecla as she sat in a windowsill and listened to the teachings of the apostle Paul. According to her mother's descriptive flourish, Thecla, "clinging to the window like a spider, lays hold of what is said by him with a strange eagerness and fearful emotion." It was for me as it had been for Thecla.

Longtime readers as well as those encountering Walter's words for the first time will discover in the volumes of the Walter Brueggemann Library the same soaring rhetoric, engaging intelligence, acute social analysis, moral clarity, wit, generosity, and grace that make it so enlightening and enjoyable to learn from and with Walter Brueggemann. The world we inhabit is broken, dominated by the special interests of the wealthy, teeming with misinformation, divided by entrenched social hierarchies, often despairing before looming ecological catastrophe, and callously indifferent, if not aggressively predatory, toward those facing increasing deprivation and immiseration.

In these volumes readers will find Walter at his best, sharply naming these dynamics of brokenness and richly engaging biblical traditions to uncover and chart alternative forms of collective life that promise to be more just, more merciful, and more loving.

Each volume in the Walter Brueggemann Library coheres around a distinct theme that is a prominent concern across Walter's many publications. The contents of the volumes consist of materials taken from a variety of his previously published works. In other words, I have compiled whole chapters or articles, sections, snippets for some volumes, and at times even just a line or two from Walter's publications, and sought to weave them together to create a new book that coheres around a specific theme, in this case the theme of worship in the book of Psalms.

We have learned immensely from Walter Brueggemann's numerous publications on the content as well as the consequences of biblical worship. Among the many biblical texts that he has considered, Brueggemann unsurprisingly focuses especially on the Psalms, about which he has written extensively.[1] While acknowledging that Brueggemann's contributions are many and various, one can begin to grasp his influence on our understandings of biblical worship, and of the Psalms in particular, from three distinct angles.

First, Brueggemann's work emphasizes the potential power contained in our language and practices of worship to construct, order, and shape the reality in which we live (see especially chaps. 2–5, 8, 9, and 12). Brueggemann embraces and exhorts readers to appreciate the extent to which language provides the medium that brings humans into relationship with one another in formal, composed social relations and institutions. With the crucial caveat that no particular social order is necessary, fixed, or natural, Brueggemann encourages readers to consider and be more intentional about how the language and practices of worship shape our communal relations, contribute to our ideas about God, and serve as a foundation for various values and commitments. From this perspective, worship is the arena through which communities can strive to create more justice and contribute to more flourishing in ways that better reflect the church's understanding of the gospel.

It is worth mentioning briefly that Brueggemann's analysis and embrace of the constitutive power of liturgy runs counter to certain prevailing trends in the humanities that have only strengthened in the years since he first published these ideas. Much humanistic scholarship has been devoted to placing value on particularity, celebrating instability, and privileging decomposition—in short, the ways in which systems and collectives inevitably come apart. These developments render Brueggemann's embrace of the structuring, formalizing, and constitutive power of liturgy even more important. While attention should be paid to the ways that our constructed and formalized social and political relationships can break down, involve exclusions, instill hierarchies, and so on, complete formlessness in human communities is not an ideal worthy of aspiration. Brueggemann helps us understand how and why we should analyze and appreciate the extent to which our language and liturgies build relationships, create spaces, and shape orders in ways that can be more or less deliberate, just, compassionate, inclusive, faithful, and so on.

Second and relatedly, Brueggemann is uniquely attentive to social and political dynamics related to worship and the content of the Psalms. I imagine that these parts of the following chapters may be most surprising to readers who are new to Brueggemann's work. Most of us probably do not think about religious worship as a political act, much less as a radically subversive political activity. And yet this is a central argument in the following chapters (see especially chaps. 3–5, 9, and 12). Moreover, Brueggemann explains why he thinks that the Psalms and biblical worship are politically subversive, not only in the context of ancient Israel, but also and even especially in the contemporary context of (most of) his readers. The act of worshiping the biblical God inevitably entails the neglect if not outright rejection of alternative authorities that compete for our loyalty. And the Psalms are filled with protest, complaint, and lament, often about issues that are public, political, and economic.

The Psalms articulate a pervasive public agenda to which God is inextricably linked. This public agenda unfolds dynamically over the course of the Psalms, and while it is not articulated in systematic terms in any single text, it consistently reflects a vision of the world as an interdependent place in which all human, natural, and social formations not only depend upon God but are also mutually conditioned. Thus, whether in lament about injustice, complaint about violence or impoverishment, or in thanksgiving for deliverance and abundance, God is entangled in the public and personal, and in human and nonhuman affairs, throughout the Psalter. Brueggemann also shows how these aspects of the Psalms function to set into relief the social issues, policy commitments, and economic arrangements of contemporary readers. Furthermore, as developed most extensively in chapter 9, communities that fail to provide space for the robust expression, recognition, and thus the legitimation of the dark sides of the Psalms—that is, lament, complaint, protest, imprecation—will, perforce, neglect if not censure the thorny issues and tough questions about social and political justice that underlie these expressions.

Third and finally, much of Brueggemann's work is informed by his breakthrough insight linking the findings of literary scholars about the different forms or genres of the Psalms with the philosopher Paul Ricoeur's observations about the seasonal flux of lived, human experience. Ricoeur suggests that human lives tend to settle in periods of relative stability or orientation, until they are inevitably disrupted by some disorienting event, out of which, eventually, we may find our lives newly oriented. Brueggemann perceives that these seasons roughly correspond to the three main types of psalms: songs of praise (orientation), lamentation (disorientation), and thanksgiving (new orientation). These seasons of life do not determine the use or efficacy of a particular type of psalm. Instead, Brueggemann suggests that seasons of orientation might incline one toward psalms of praise, disorientation toward laments, and new orientation toward thanksgiving. (Incidentally, this explains my organization of this volume into three parts, following the more general introductory essays in part 1.) But one need not be in a season of disorientation to utter a lament, and the utterance of a lament can, functionally, orient an individual or community toward the life circumstances that might lead one to write or identify with words of lamentation, protest, and complaint. Brueggemann's typology is also functional in the sense that it permits us to consider how a particular (type of) psalm might impact individuals and communities, and—especially in chapter 9 as mentioned above—how the neglect or prohibition of a particular (type of) psalm could have costly consequences for individuals and communities.

The chapters in this book are only a sample of the many contributions that Brueggemann has made to our collective understanding of worship in the biblical tradition. They reflect and elaborate these three, rather flexible, areas of Brueggemann's interest, and also venture into other questions and concerns related to worship in the Bible. I hope this volume will urge readers to explore Brueggemann's work on this topic further. Even more, I hope that it will incite in readers a desire to form new social bonds through worship practices, develop richer experiences and deeper passions in any and every season of readers' lives, and energize communities of faith to recognize injustices and create and advocate for more just, healthy, and flourishing forms of collective life.

I am grateful to numerous people for their encouragement and help. First on the list is Walter Brueggemann, whose faith in and patience with me has begun to seem endless, even as I know that it must demand great effort and care at times. Also, I continue to admire the wise and supportive team at Westminster John Knox— and only in part because they are so good at making my work better! In particular, the energy, editorial gifts, and passionate convictions that Julie Mullins so graciously brings to her projects are infectious and truly joyful.

For the past five years I have benefited and learned much from the leadership and lucid mind of my department chair, Kevin Schilbrack. Kevin, the College of Arts and Sciences, and Appalachian State University have continued to provide me with support and encouragement on this and many other projects. I feel deeply fortunate for the help and contributions of many colleagues, family, and friends over the past few pandemic-filled and exceedingly difficult years. To list any seems a slight to many, but I should warmly thank Brennan Breed, Rick Elmore, Kelly Murphy, Brent Strawn, Roger Nam, Sylvie Honigman, Pearce Hayes, Joe Weiss, Kathy Beach, Grimes Thomas, Francis Landy, Carol Newsom, and Joe and Sara Evans. In different ways, each has been an irreplaceable companion and source of inspiration.

Finally, I want to thank my family, immediate and extended, and especially my wife, Stephanie, to whom I remain exceedingly indebted. If on any particular day I am inspired, insightful, funny, or passionate, it is surely because of Stephanie and our children's incredible, joyful, and beautiful companionship. While my heart still waits, my capacity for full-throated lament and praise is undoubtedly made possible by these and many other gracious comrades journeying alongside me.

Davis Hankins
Appalachian State University
Spring 2022

PART ONE

Worship in the Bible

Chapter 1

Introduction to the Book of Psalms

When we come to the question of worship in the Bible, the book of Psalms is unquestionably the indispensable starting point. The book of Psalms, complex in its formation and pluralistic in its content, is Israel's highly stylized, normative script for dialogical covenantalism, designed for many "reperformances":

- It is *complex in its formation* because the psalms seem to arise from many variant settings in diverse times, places, and circumstances. The collection of Psalms, moreover, is itself a collection of subcollections, at least some of which were extant before the book itself was formed.
- It is *pluralistic in its content*, reflecting many different sources and advocacies, so a rich diversity of theological voices is offered in it.
- It is *highly stylized*, so that there are predictable speech patterns that become, through usage, familiar. These patterns can be identified according to rhetorical genres that reflect characteristic usage. As a result, it appears that certain patterns of speech are intimately and regularly connected to certain kinds of human experience and circumstance. As a consequence, one may, with some imagination, read backward from speech patterns to social contexts.
- It is *designed for reperformance*. The Psalms offer expressions of praise and prayer that have been found, over generations, to be recurringly poignant and pertinent to the ebb and flow of human life. Generations of Jews and Christians have found

the Psalms to be a reliable resource for the articulation of faith, but also for the authentic articulation of life in its complexity. Along with usage in worship, the Psalms have been reperformed as instruction, as the young have been socialized and inculcated into the lifeworld of the Psalms that includes both buoyant hope and a summoning ethic that belong to this singing, praying community.

• The book serves *dialogic covenantalism.* The praise and prayer expressed therein assume and affirm that this is a real transaction: there is a God on the other end of the singing and speaking. The two partners, Israel and YHWH, are bound in mutual loyalty and obligation. This relationship refuses both parties autonomy without responsible connection, and yet requires defining self-assertion without subservient submission. Thus the practice of the Psalter protects the community from both religious temptations of negating the reality of God and negating the legitimacy of the life of the community.

Two Psalmic Extremities

Gratitude and Praise

We may identify two stylized speech patterns that serve to voice, in the congregation and in the presence of God, the extremities of human experience. Many of these psalms are affirmative expressions of *gratitude* offered as thanks and exuberance and awe offered as *praise.* In these psalms attention is completely ceded over to the wonder of God, who is celebrated as the giver of good gifts and the faithful, gracious governor of all reality. These speech-songs constitute a glad affirmation that the center of faithful existence rests not with human persons or human achievements, but with the God who is known in the normative narrative memory of Israel. Such hymns of praise regularly attest to God's character as in the briefest of the Psalms:

> For great is his steadfast love toward us,
>   and the faithfulness of the LORD endures forever.
> Ps. 117:2a

The two characteristics of YHWH celebrated here are "steadfast love" and "faithfulness," two synonyms for YHWH's readiness to honor covenantal commitments to Israel and to the world.

Along with attestation concerning YHWH's character, many hymns celebrate the marvelous "wonders" of YHWH—wonders committed on some specific occasion and those regularly performed by Israel's Lord. Thus, in Psalm 146:3–9, the capacity of YHWH to enact social transformations is contrasted with that of "princes," who have no energy or capacity for such transformations. The vista of YHWH's action is as large as creation itself. But the accent of the psalm is YHWH's commitment to the well-being of the socially vulnerable and marginal, which is to say, prisoners, those who are blind, those who are bowed down, strangers, orphans, widows, all those who are without conventional social protection. In this characterization of God, the psalm already articulates an ethical summons to God's followers that they too are to be engaged with such vulnerable and marginal persons.

One of the richest deposits of such hymns of praise is at the conclusion of the Psalter in Psalms 146–150, in which the particulars of psalmic praise wane, and the exuberance of praise becomes more vigorous and bolder. In Psalm 148, the singers can imagine all creation, all creatures, including sea monsters and creeping things, united in praise of YHWH. By the culmination of the sequence in Psalm 150, there is a total lack of any specificity, and users of the psalm are invited to dissolve in a glad self-surrender that is to be enacted in the most lyrical way imaginable. Such praise is a recognition that the wonder and splendor of this God—known in the history of Israel and in the beauty of creation—pushes beyond our explanatory categories, so that there can be only a liturgical, emotive rendering of all creatures before the creator.

The gladness of thanksgiving matches the exuberance of praise, only there is much more specificity in the articulation of thanksgiving. Those who are thankful can "count their blessings" and identify the gifts of God. Thus in Psalm 116 the speaker can remember and recount the prayers of petition previously uttered in a circumstance of need (vv. 1–3). The "snares of death" refers to some circumstance in which the speaker was left helpless. But now, after the crisis, the speaker has been "delivered" by God (v. 8) and is restored to "the land of the living," that is, to full bodily well-being and social acceptance (v. 9).

This psalm indicates that the utterance of thanksgiving is done in a liturgical setting in which appropriate action would have accompanied the utterance. Thus the speaker remembers having pledged an offering to God if delivered and now "pays my vow," a "thanksgiving sacrifice." This is an act of gratitude and at the same time testimony to the congregation that God has indeed performed a wondrous deliverance that runs beyond all categories of self-sufficiency.

Lament and Complaint

The other primary genre of prayer, at the other emotional extremity, consists in lament and complaint. In these psalms, the speaker petitions YHWH for help in a circumstance of desperate need. Whereas in praise the speaker has gladly *ceded self* over to the wonder of God, in these laments the speaker *claims self*, asserts self amid acute need, and presumes self-legitimacy in expecting God's ready deliverance. Whereas the songs of praise and thanks are dominated by the language of "you," these prayers are dominated by first-person pronouns in which the central subject of preoccupation is not God, but the needy, trusting, demanding "I." Consider, for example, Psalm 77:

> I cry aloud to God,
>> aloud to God, that he may hear me.
> In the day of my trouble I seek the Lord;
>> in the night my hand is stretched out without wearying;
>> my soul refuses to be comforted.
> I think of God, and I moan;
>> I meditate, and my spirit faints.
>
> vv. 1–3

The language in this instance is intimately personal. But the genre of lament and complaint can also include public crises that concern the entire community. This may refer variously to drought, war, or, quintessentially, the destruction of Jerusalem. In Psalm 44, the community employs assaulting rhetoric in addressing God for being abusive and neglectful. In verses 9–14, the language is dominated by an accusatory "you." But the "us" on the receiving end of alleged divine (mis)conduct is the accent point in the psalm. All that matters is what has happened to "us." The rhetoric is against God, accusing God of reneging on promises of fidelity.

Two Theological Foci

Beyond the two psalmic extremities, two theological foci that run through the Psalter can also be identified, each of which is announced at the beginning of the book.

Torah Obedience and the Promise of *Shalom*

In Psalm 1, the accent is on Torah, the urgency of obedience to Torah as the promise of *shalom* that comes with such obedience. It is clear that this theme reflects the symmetry of the tradition of the book of Deuteronomy, the normative covenantal tradition that is derived from Mount Sinai. It is the core claim of that tradition that obedience to Torah is a way of life, and disobedience to Torah is a way of death (see, e.g., Deut. 30:15–20). The conclusion of Psalm 1 is an assertion of such a conviction:

> Therefore the wicked will not stand in the judgment,
>   nor sinners in the congregation of the righteous;
> for the LORD watches over the way of the righteous,
>   but the way of the wicked will perish.
>
> Ps. 1:5–6

The same theme is reflected in the ethical catalogs of Psalms 15, 24, and 112. But it is also assumed in the laments that voice an expectation of an entitlement that is rooted in covenantal obedience. The tradition confirms that the world is ethically guaranteed and reliable, due to God's fidelity. The problem, so evident in the laments, is that lived experience tells otherwise, and so Israel can pray to YHWH in abrasive and demanding ways.

Jerusalem, David, and the Temple

The second theme is focused on the Jerusalem establishment that hosts both the Davidic dynasty and the temple. Psalm 2 is placed at the outset of the Psalter to express the significance of David and his dynasty for the faith of Israel. This tradition celebrates YHWH's unconditional promise to David. That promise is seen to have failed in Psalm 89, a psalm whose subject is David:

> But now you have spurned and rejected him;
> > you are full of wrath against your anointed.
> You have renounced the covenant with your servant;
> > you have defiled his crown in the dust. . . .
> Lord, where is your steadfast love of old,
> > which by your faithfulness you swore to David?
>
> > > 89:38–39, 49

In Psalm 132, moreover, the unconditional promise to David (see 2 Sam. 7:11–16) has been subsumed to the conditional promise of Sinai. Now the promise depends on Torah obedience:

> The LORD swore to David a sure oath
> > from which he will not turn back:
> "One of the sons of your body
> > I will set on your throne.
> If your sons keep my covenant
> > and my decrees that I shall teach them,
> their sons also, forevermore,
> > shall sit on your throne."
>
> > > Ps. 132:11–12

It is also possible to see in other "royal psalms" that the Psalter continues to take YHWH's commitment to David seriously, a commitment that eventuates in Jewish and Christian messianism.

This Jerusalem tradition also pertains to the temple, which is the epitome of an ordered world. So we have "Songs of Zion" in the Psalter that celebrate the city of Jerusalem and the temple as the epicenter of cosmic reality. The best known of these Zion songs is Psalm 46, which celebrates the assured presence of God in the city, even in the face of instability and the threat of chaos. The Songs of Ascent in Psalms 120–134, a now distinct subcollection in the Psalter, were perhaps pilgrim songs initially sung by those in religious procession on their way to the temple. These include Psalm 121, which is in the voice of a traveler at risk, and Psalm 122, which speaks of going up "to the house of the LORD." Many of these psalms bear the residue of actual liturgical practice.

These several hymnic enhancements of Jerusalem are matched and countered by psalms that reflect on and respond to the destruction of Jerusalem at the hands of Babylon in 587 BCE. Thus Psalm 74:4–8 describes in some painful detail the way in which invading forces have violated the temple. Better known is Psalm 137, in which the deportees from Jerusalem are taunted to sing "a song of Zion" in a foreign land. While some might doubt that the phrase "Song of Zion" in Psalm 137 is a technical phrase, it nevertheless most likely refers to a corpus of psalms (Pss. 46, 48, 76, 84) and others like them that celebrated the temple. Taken together, these Songs of Zion and the laments over the temple and the city dramatize the hold the temple held on Israel's imagination. In Christian usage, moreover, the loss of the temple and the rebuilding of the temple in the Persian period were transposed so that they became a way of speaking about the crucifixion and resurrection of Jesus (see John 2:18–22).

The Shape of the Psalter

Finally, it may be noted that the Psalter is divided into five distinct "books," each of which culminates with a sweeping doxology. Interpreters presently are considering clues that suggest that these several "books" may have been formed as they are by design, so that the sequence of psalms is not random but aims, in itself, to make a theological statement. In such a hypothesis, each psalm is placed strategically to serve the larger whole. The five books are, perhaps, designed as a match for and reflection of the five books of Moses (Genesis–Deuteronomy), Israel's most normative literature. Seen in this light, the Psalter is always an echo of that normative tradition. And while Christians are often tempted to overlook the particularity of the Psalms and to transpose them into a more generic spirituality, in fact this psalmic poetry belongs to the particularity of this specific Israelite community of praise and prayer. And as the church took over the Psalter for its own use in worship and instruction, it has reread it with reference to the Gospel claims of Jesus of Nazareth.

Taken in largest sweep, the Psalms move from the summons to Torah in Psalm 1 to the doxological self-abandonment of Psalms 146–150. The God who commands Torah is the God who exercises generative sovereignty over all creation. The convergence of urgent summons, candid response, and doxological self-abandonment is altogether appropriate within a covenantal relationship. The Psalter is thus a script for that continuing relationship. And whenever we perform that script, we commit a countercultural act, counter to the dominant political, epistemological, and symbolic assumptions of our culture. This thick poetry goes deeply beneath and boldly beyond our usual rationality, so that such performance may yield access to the reality of God's own holiness.

The Primary Character of the Psalter

The chapters that follow elaborate various ways in which the world freshly mediated by the Psalms opposes the world that has shaped us and to which we cling. For the rest of this chapter, I focus on the Primary Character that makes the counterworld of the Psalms so different and compelling in contrast to our closely held world. This Primary Character is YHWH, and YHWH is a lively character and a real agent of firm resolve who brings transformative energy and emancipatory capacity to all our social transactions.

I will draw the contrast as starkly as I can. The world we hold closely is "without God," that is, without the god attested in the script of the Psalms. To be sure, our closely held world is not without its god or gods, but it is definitely without this God. We may characterize the available gods of our closely held world as idols, the ones described in Psalm 115:

> They have mouths, but do not speak;
>   eyes, but do not see.
> They have ears, but do not hear;
>   noses, but do not smell.
> They have hands, but do not feel;

feet, but do not walk;
they make no sound in their throats.

vv. 5–7

These gods are objects and not subjects; they are not agents, not
capable of transformative action. In the words of Isaiah's mock
address to these gods, "do good, or do harm, that we may be afraid
and terrified. You, indeed, are nothing and your work is nothing at
all" (Isa. 41:23b–24a).

- They are the usual suspects: the gods of patriotism, nationalism,
  capitalism, and mastery of knowledge.
- They are the gods of scholastic conservatism that go under the
  banner of "evangelical," the ones so tied up in formula and prop-
  osition and logic that yield certitude that they cannot save. As
  the psalm says, they cannot "make a sound in their throats" (Ps.
  115:7) because they specialize only in immutability.
- They are the gods of progressivism who conform to Enlightenment rationality and who never bother anyone; the gods who, in
  the words of the psalm, have hands but cannot feel because, as
  the saying goes, "God has no hands but our hands."

There is a collusion here among the neo-atheists, the scholastic
reductionists, and the urbane progressives to have a god who is either
remote from all worldly reality and does not engage with us or who
is so intimate with us that we choose to be "spiritual but not religious," which means, I believe, something like: "I am not account-
able to anyone, and neither God nor I have any public staying power
in faith."

Now perhaps this is an overly stark presentation of the false gods,
but no more so than the indictment found in Psalm 115. Alongside
that poem, there are two more famous characterizations of such
divine irrelevance. In Jeremiah 10, we are treated to a Feuerbachian
manufacture of gods:

For the customs of the peoples are false:
a tree from the forest is cut down,
    and worked with an ax by the hands of an artisan;
people deck it with silver and gold;

they fasten it with hammer and nails
  so that it cannot move.
Their idols are like scarecrows in a cucumber field,
  and they cannot speak;
they have to be carried,
  for they cannot walk.
Do not be afraid of them,
  for they cannot do evil,
  nor is it in them to do good.

Jer. 10:3–5

And in Isaiah 44, there is a mocking of phony gods and those who make them:

> The ironsmith fashions it and works it over the coals, shaping it with hammers, and forging it with his strong arm; he becomes hungry and his strength fails, he drinks no water and is faint. The carpenter stretches a line, marks it out with a stylus, fashions it with planes, and marks it with a compass; he makes it in human form, with human beauty, to be set up in a shrine. He cuts down cedars or chooses a holm tree or an oak and lets it grow strong, among the trees of the forest. He plants a cedar and the rain nourishes it. Then it can be used as fuel. Part of it he takes and warms himself; he kindles a fire and bakes bread. Then he makes a god and worships it, makes it a carved image and bows down before it. (Isa. 44:12–15)

Worst of all, several texts observe that if one worships such gods, one becomes like them: passive and mute, nothing more than a couch-potato consumer of the National Security State:

> Those who make them are like them;
>   so are all who trust in them.

Ps. 115:8

> [They] went after worthless things, and became worthless themselves.

Jer. 2:5

> [They] consecrated themselves to a thing of shame,
> and became detestable like the thing they loved.

Hos. 9:10

I focus on the theme of "without god" because I want to underscore that the counterworld of the Psalms witnesses to and makes available a God of agency, who shatters the serene sedation of our closely held world. This witness and availability happen only in, with, and under this script—by word, song, dramatic performance, responsive litany, and all the ways in which our closely held world of control and failure is broken open. Thus, the scripting of the Psalms is a subversive act that intends to undo the dominant version of reality. Through the words, phrases, images, and metaphors given there, we receive an odd alternative that requires us to reconsider our closely held world. The Psalms mediate to us the leading character of the creator God who will judge the living and the dead; the covenant-making God of Israel who waxes and wanes in presence and absence, in fidelity and infidelity, who comes, we say, enfleshed at Nazareth, and so is preoccupied with matters of the flesh, with life and death, with wealth and poverty, with wisdom and foolishness, with power and weakness, with beginning and ending and endings and beginnings—the deep, thick stuff of life in the world that cannot be given in memos or syllogisms, but only in narrative and in poem.

The Psalter, in a word, is a God-occupied corpus, which leads to at least seven crucial observations:

The Earth Will Yield Its Fruit

1. The Psalms invite us to trust and so move away from anxiety about scarcity, precisely because this is *the God of abundance*, who gives freely and without limit. It is the assurance of this God that the earth will yield its fruit in due season:

> As long as the earth endures,
>   seedtime and harvest, cold and heat,
> summer and winter, day and night,
>   shall not cease.
>
> Gen. 8:22

A New Testament exhibit of this guarantee is the twelve baskets of loaves left over, because "your heavenly Father knows that you need all these things" (Matt. 6:32). But without this God we are left in scarcity and in endless anxiety.

God Prepares a Table

2. The Psalms invite us to generosity, not greed, because this is the God who *prepares a table* for us in the presence of our enemies (see Pss. 23:5; 78:19). This God is always setting the table of abundance, always preparing more, always supplying bread for those who are hungry, always cooking fish on the seashore, always setting a welcome table for the stranger, the widow, and the orphan:

> You cause the grass to grow for the cattle,
>   and plants for people to use,
> to bring forth food from the earth,
>   and wine to gladden the human heart,
> oil to make the face shine,
>   and bread to strengthen the human heart.
>   Ps. 104:14–15

How striking that this ancient doxology on creation can name the central elements of sacramental life:

> *wine* to gladden the heart;
> *oil* to make the face shine;
> *bread* to strengthen the human heart.

It is always these three—wine, oil, and bread: wine poured out like blood, bread broken like body, oil to anoint the dying and the baptized. Wine, oil, bread—these are the stuff of life, the stuff of sacrament, the stuff of sign.

Without the God given in this script, there may be wine, but it is likely our own product; there may be bread, but we baked it; there may be oil, but we squeezed it from the olives. And when we produce, bake, and squeeze, there is never enough, and we must hoard. But this script has always known that this wine, bread, and oil are gifts—gifts beyond our effort, gifts that, like grits and like grace, "just come."

A Summons to Trust

3. The Psalms summon us to *trust another* and to give up our desperate self-sufficiency. In a world without God, we had better be adequately self-sufficient, because in that world there is no free

lunch. But this God breaks the need for and the possibility of self-sufficiency. Thus, in Psalm 73, the speaker envies those who are rich, powerful, and cynical their endless successful prosperity. But when he goes to the sanctuary, to the place where the Psalms are recited, he comes abruptly to a double awareness. On the one hand, he concludes that the cynically self-sufficient cannot endure:

> Truly you set them in slippery places;
> you make them fall to ruin.
> How they are destroyed in a moment,
> swept away utterly by terrors!
> They are like a dream when one awakes;
> on awakening you despise their phantoms.
> Ps. 73:18–20

On the other hand, the psalmist comes to the recognition that the weapons of self-sufficiency no longer have any attraction for him, because he is now attracted only to the God of life and fidelity:

> Whom have I in heaven but you?
> And there is nothing on earth that I desire other than you.
> My flesh and my heart may fail,
> but God is the strength of my heart and my portion forever.
> vv. 25–26

This script invites us to move from the world of commodities that will never give us life, to the world of communion in which Another Presence is more than adequate for our life in the world.

God the Truth-Teller

4. As elaborated in later chapters, the Psalms script us for truth-telling that breaks the killing force of denial. It is no surprise, then, that it is the *truth-telling God* who first told the truth about us:

> Do not fear, for I have redeemed you;
> I have called you by name, you are mine.
> Isa. 43:1

That is the bottom-line truth of our existence. Or in the wondrous words of the Heidelberg Catechism, "That I belong to my faithful savior, Jesus Christ." That I belong! That I belong to Another. This defining truth is what permits us to tell our own truth, and we are heard into newness. In our closely held world, we dare not risk telling the truth, because it will not be heard; or, even if it is heard, it will not be honored, and may even be used against us.

But not in the Psalms, because this God is a listener. So we tell our secrets in the holy presence. The psalmist describes the high cost of silent denial:

> While I kept silence, my body wasted away
>   through my groaning all day long.
> For day and night your hand was heavy upon me;
>   My strength was dried up as by the heat of summer.
>
> Ps. 32:3–4

But emancipatory healing came through truth-telling:

> Then I acknowledged my sin to you,
>   and I did not hide my iniquity;
> I said, "I will confess my transgressions to the LORD,"
>   and you forgave the guilt of my sin.
>
> v. 5

This practice of speaking and hearing is richly attested in the laments, in the full articulation of our life before the one from whom no secrets are hid. When we practice such disclosure, we find that in having our truths heard and known, we are transformed and empowered to new life and well-being. This was, of course, the great insight of Freud in the twentieth century, but it was no accident that Freud was a Jew who knew this script. And as Freud confounded the Victorian world of Vienna, so also this truth-telling and the God who hears it always confound our closely held world of denial.

God the Promise-Keeper

5. The Psalms mediate to us the great *promise-keeper* whose resolve guarantees that the world is not a closed system. Creation, instead, is a world very much in process, sure to come to full *shalom*. Despair is the fate of a world "without god," where there are no new gifts to be given. The Psalms refuse that world, knowing that God is not yet

finished. Consequently, the Psalms can gather all the great words of
the covenant and apply them to the future:

> Steadfast love and faithfulness will meet;
>   righteousness and peace will kiss each other.
> Faithfulness will spring up from the ground,
>   and righteousness will look down from the sky.
> The LORD will give what is good,
>   and our land will yield its increase.
> Righteousness will go before him,
>   and will make a path for his steps.
>
> Ps. 85:10–13

Here the entire vocabulary of fidelity is thrown toward the future—
steadfast love, faithfulness, righteousness, peace, faithfulness twice,
righteousness three times—all in the "will" of the not-yet.

At the center of this hope is YHWH: "The LORD will give." Psalm
85 imagines the steps of this God into a future of well-being. As a
result of that divine resolve, the earth will yield and yield and yield.
There is more to come, and it is good. There is more to come because
God said, long before Martin Luther King Jr., "I have a dream," a
dream of *shalom*. We live toward that dream because God's dream
will not be defeated.

Community of Deep Memory

6. The Psalms exhibit *a community of deep memory*, a memory of
fidelity, transformation, and miracle; a memory, moreover, that
becomes present reality and passionate possibility. What God has
done, God will do. Thus, in the psalmic expression of Lamentations
3, the poet describes how Israel in exile had lost all hope. But then
there is a stunning reversal by means of memory:

> But this I call to mind,
>   and therefore I have hope:
> the steadfast love of the LORD never ceases,
>   his mercies never come to an end;
> they are new every morning;
>   great is your faithfulness.
>
> Lam. 3:21–23

In the script, Israel continually and consistently meets to recite the steadfast love, faithfulness, and mercy of God. Israel names names and times and circumstances and specificities. And Israel knows that what is remembered presses into contemporary life, so that present life, like remembered life, is an arena for fidelity with and before God.

It comes as no surprise, then, that God is the great rememberer:

> He has remembered his great love and faithfulness
>   to the house of Israel.
> All the ends of the earth have seen
>   the victory of our God.
>
> Ps. 98:3

> As a father has compassion for his children,
>   so the LORD has compassion for those who fear him.
> For he knows how we were made;
>   he remembers that we are dust.
>
> 103:13–14

The reference to dust harkens back to Genesis 2: God remembers the moment of creation when we were formed of earthly fragility. And out of that divine remembering, God has compassion like that of a parent for a child.

To be sure, this God has a delete button, but it is for the deletion of offenses:

> Have mercy on me, O God,
>   according to your steadfast love;
> according to your abundant mercy,
>   blot out my transgressions.
>
> Ps. 51:1

This delete button is all about "blotting out" transgression. This God, with great freedom, works toward our best selves and our best world, deleting what must be forgotten, remembering what must be treasured and reperformed. It is precisely because of this divine freedom that God's world is so different from our closely held one, which is so permeated by amnesia that nothing precious can be treasured. That is why we meet regularly, with script in hand, to "do this in remembrance."

A Light Yoke and Easy Burden

7. The summons of the Psalms is always again to Sinai, not in order to impose legalism, but to ponder *a light yoke and an easy burden* that is an alternative to the hard yoke and heavy burden of our closely held world of relentless deadlines and constant productivity. When we engage the Psalms, we go again to Sinai, where the mystery of viable life is delivered. The Psalms begin with a reference to Sinai:

> Happy are those
> > who do not follow the advice of the wicked,
> or take the path that sinners tread,
> > or sit in the seats of scoffers;
> but their delight is in the law of the LORD,
> > and on his law they meditate day and night.
>
> 1:1–2

A normed life is like a willow tree, like a banquet, like a dance, like a journey home. The norms from the mountain are given by God. They are firm and nonnegotiable. Yet they are always under interpretation and reformulation.

The foolish, unnormed life, of course, is not so. Fools never make it to Sinai; they think there is no god; they think they can do as they wish without destroying self or neighbor. But we who read the Psalms know better. The counterworld found there is not a jungle. There, might does not make right, and our life has more than a private meaning. No, in the Psalms we are lined out as our best selves:

> Praise the LORD!
> > Happy are those who fear the LORD,
> > who greatly delight in his commandments.
> Their descendants will be mighty in the land;
> > the generation of the upright will be blessed.
> Wealth and riches are in their houses,
> > and their faithfulness endures forever.
> They rise in the darkness as a light for the upright;
> > they are gracious, merciful, and righteous.
> It is well with those who deal generously and lend,
> > who conduct their affairs with justice.
> For the righteous will never be moved;
> > they will be remembered forever.

They are not afraid of evil tidings;
    their hearts are firm, secure in the LORD.

112:1–7

It is the work of the Psalter to populate our world with the character of this God. Where this God governs, the world is transformed and transformable. It becomes a place of joy and duty—of joyous duty—a place of buoyancy and risk. Even so, we itch to be left in a joyless, duty-free world that is noticeably short on buoyancy and empty of serious risk. But because we have entered this counterworld, we may decide differently. The people of this counterworld of covenantal duty and joy, of buoyancy and risk, will now and in time to come be characteristically lost in wonder, love, and praise.

Questions for Reflection

1. The reperformance of psalms in worship allows participants to articulate faith as well as articulate the complexity of life. Are there particular psalms—or verses from psalms—that have given voice to your own articulation of praise, lament, and faith as you have experienced them? What were the settings and occasions?

2. What does it mean to you that the Psalms assume and affirm that there is a God on the other end of our singing and speaking in worship and prayer? Brueggemann calls this "dialogic covenantalism." What would you call it?

3. The Psalms give us a countercultural script, as we compare our closely held world that recognizes no god but idols (like patriotism, nationalism, capitalism, scholastic conservatism, progressivism, etc.), with the creative, covenant-making, deeply engaged God of the Psalter. What evidence do you see of a worldview "without God" in your local community? How comfortable are you with the idea of being "countercultural" as you affirm the faith of the Psalms in worship?

4. Which of the seven observations about the Psalms described on pages 13–20, and listed below, particularly resonates with you today? Which do you most need to remember? Which does your worshiping community as a whole most need to remember?

- The Earth Will Yield Its Fruit (celebrating abundance over scarcity)
- God Prepares a Table (recognizing generosity over greed)
- A Summons to Trust (trusting each other and God over self-sufficiency)
- God the Truth-Teller (speaking truth over denial)
- God the Promise-Keeper (a dream of *shalom* over despair)
- Community of Deep Memory (recalling God's past fidelity over amnesia)
- A Light Yoke and Easy Burden (following God's law over normlessness)

Chapter 2

Praise as a Constitutive Act

Praise is the duty and delight, the ultimate vocation of the human community; indeed, of all creation.[1] Here I want to articulate the full importance of that vocation, which is both duty and delight. To be sure, praise is addressed to heaven. But it is equally true that praise is spoken by human voices on earth. Inevitably then, praise is not a pure, unmitigated impingement in heaven. The act also impinges on earth. That is, praise is not only a religious vocation, but it is also a social gesture that effects the shape and character of human life and human community.

I want to pay attention to the social reality of praise, so that we might discern more fully its theological risk and benefit. I do not minimize the genuinely theological character of the act of praise, but I want to approach it critically, in order that our practice of worship and our commitment to ethical responsibility should be intentionally related to each other. My argument is based on the conviction that the church has acute problems concerning ethical responsibility because our worship has not been critiqued or understood as a social act. As a result, we find ourselves embracing realities about which we are not intentional. Worship in which heaven and earth commune is worship in which our deepest religious acts and our boldest worldly commitments may be brought under a common discipline.

The Psalms as Creative Acts

In addition to being responsive to the reality, power, and activity of God, praise is also *constitutive* of theological reality. It not only

23

addresses the God who is there before us, but also is an act of constructing the theological world in which we shall interact with God. Because praise is *constitutive* as well as *responsive*, practitioners of praise would do well to be critical, knowing, and intentional about the enterprise of construction.

The magisterial hypothesis of Sigmund Mowinckel is the beginning point of our study. In 1921–24, Mowinckel wrote six short studies on the Psalms.[2] Of the six fascicles of his original work, it is the second that concerns us. The formal title, which indicates Mowinckel's concern for the relation between worship and eschatology, is "The Festival of the Enthronement of Yahweh, and the Origin of Eschatology."[3]

In an incredibly imaginative act, Mowinckel proposed that in the early days of the Jerusalem temple, the king sponsored and supervised a festival. In the festival YHWH was once again enthroned as sovereign for the coming year. The regularized and routinized liturgical sequence of the festival provided for a ritual combat among various gods, all of whom wanted to be king. Thus the premise of the hypothesis is a vigorous polytheism. YHWH, the God of Israel, was victorious in combat and so warranted the throne. There was then a celebrative procession in which YHWH ascended the throne and was acclaimed king. The other gods promised to serve and obey this God for a year. Seated upon the throne, YHWH gave something like a "state of the union" message, in which the condition of life was decreed for the coming year. It was characteristically a decree of health, peace, and *shalom*. Mowinckel proposed (and Aubrey Johnson reinforced) the notion that the Davidic king played a crucial role in the festival.[4] The king, according to the hypothesis, played the role of YHWH and was enthroned on his behalf. That is, the enthronement of YHWH as God carried with it important implications for the legitimacy of the Davidic monarchy, which was also liturgically renewed in the festival.

That Mowinckel's title also concerned eschatology has gone largely unnoticed among scholars. He proposed that eschatology is a projection of hope into the future out of a cultic enactment that never fully met expectations. The term "cultic" here and in most references to ancient religious practices does not mean anything marginal or unusual, but rather derives from the Latin word for "care" and refers generally to any part of how a religious system "cares" for a deity, figure, or object (as in *viticulture* for "grape care"). Because present realities were short of the expectations proclaimed in the cultic enactment, Israel's hope was delayed and increasingly displaced by the future.[5] That is, the cultic act, which is an act of liturgic imagination, opens to a future that was in tension with "business as usual." In that context, the very enactment of the narrative (*mythos*) of the cult is itself an assertion of an alternative world that permits a basis for hope.[6] All such liturgic activity is thus an act that critiques the present world and embraces an alternative future that would be liberated from it.

The Constitutive Power of Praise

Mowinckel's hypothesis has not yet been fully considered, because attention has focused on the wrong place. Criticism has attended to questions about kingship and evidence for the particulars of the festival, but that mostly misses the point. What counts is that the cult (and therefore, praise) is understood by Mowinckel as *constitutive* and not merely *responsive*. It is not as important to focus on the substance of kingship as on the claim that in public worship Israel is engaged in constructing a world in which Israel can viably, joyously, and obediently live.

If the cult is creative, then what was done in the cult is constructive. What was done in the cult was praise. Praise not only celebrates God but portrays the world given us by this God now received as sovereign. From this celebration of God and portrayal of world, we may ask, *in what sense is praise constitutive of the world?* I suggest that the constitutive power of praise is anthropologically and sociologically a most plausible, attractive, and finally, important idea.[7]

I take up this question of creative cult and constitutive praise because I believe the matter is of interest and importance to the exercise of the pastoral office. My interest is not speculative, but intensely practical. To the extent that praise, and worship more generally, is constitutive, awareness of this constitutive element will permit greater intentionality and will permit the agents of liturgical drama—pastors and leaders—to be more knowingly critical of what they themselves do. As long as cultic acts of praise are taken to be only responsive and not constitutive, the agents of the drama are likely to be neither intentional nor critical. Lack of such awareness in itself, however, will not prevent the inevitably ongoing work of construction.

Thus I begin with Mowinckel's notion of *worship as world-making*. Mowinckel's introduction to the question of creativity in cult may be summarized in his own words:

> Cult (*'abodah*) was for ancient Israel, as for primitive men generally, the festive, holy activities through which the divine power, the blessing (*berakah*) of the society, the community, and through it, individuals, was obtained.[8]

The operative word "obtained" (*erwerben*) is crucial. The cult effects that which would not otherwise be effected. Or again, Mowinckel asserts:

> The cult is not only originally, but everywhere and always, drama. Cult is a holy enterprise, but it is at the same time a holy reality. It is not merely a playful drama, a play, but an effective and reality-generating drama, a drama which actualizes with real power the dramatic event, a reality which shows forth real power, or in other words, a sacrament.[9]

Mowinckel's rhetoric leaves no doubt of his intention, as he repeats the word for "reality" (*Wirklichkeit*) three times in this one paragraph. The action of the sacramental drama is "real." It effects something. Mowinckel continues:

> These are the holy actions of cult. At the same time these actions maintain (*erhalten*) "the world," the cosmos. The tribal sphere and the national state of the "world" are originally and properly identical.[10]

Two matters are of interest in this statement. First, the verb "maintain" is a strong verb, again suggesting effective action. Second, the term "world" is in quotation marks, but the word "cosmos" is not. The last sentence indicates that Mowinckel means the creation and maintenance of a lifeworld and a socioeconomic-political order that makes public life possible and sustainable. That formation of a viable lifeworld happens through the work of the cult. The identification of world and cosmos with a social lifeworld will be important for our argument.

Notice that Mowinckel is not suggesting that cult *ought* to do this creative work, nor indeed that the cult *ought not* to do this. It simply does, as every serious pastor knows. Every serious pastor knows as they listen to parishioners that what happens in sacramental activity has a reality that outsiders do not understand, but that nonetheless is a reality. The problem is not in the character of the cultic act, but in our poor language, which can scarcely say what it is that we do, and in our poor epistemology, which can scarcely know what it is that we do.

Taken as an anthropological statement, Mowinckel's analysis may be simply descriptive: This is how the cult operates. Taken as a theological statement, one may claim that cult, as a gift from God, is granted as a means through which God's creative power is mediated. That is what we mean when we say a sacrament is "instituted." Mowinckel would, I believe, say that the dramatic work of worship is instituted, that is, authorized and legitimated, by the power of God to do world-making work, which is God's work, but which is processed through intentional, disciplined, obedient human action and human speech. It is the process of the authorized word and the legitimated action that decisively shapes and articulates the world. If the subject of liturgy is kingship—of YHWH, of David, or derivatively, of Jesus—then the liturgy serves to authorize, recognize, coronate, and legitimate the ruler and the order that belongs to that ruler. The liturgy is the festive act of enthroning and the obedient act of submitting more and more areas of life to that newly wrought sovereignty. The world may think this is subjective self-deception, but the assembly that credits the speech and action knows that the reality of God is not a reality unless it is visibly done in, with, and by the community. That is what we know, even if that knowledge flies in the face of our cynical modernity. That is what we know and attest to as professionals who preside over this action for the sake of the others, and what we know as participants as we sense our own world shaped and reshaped, maintained, renewed, transformed. What we know and see happen there we know will not happen anywhere else. Everything, therefore, is at stake in world-making here.

I wish then, if I have correctly understood Mowinckel, to suggest that the praise of Israel—or more broadly, the human vocation of praise—is to maintain and transform the world, obtain a blessing that would not be obtained, maintained, or transformed, except through this routinized and most serious activity authorized by God and enacted by human agents. "World-making" is done by God. That is foundational to Israel's faith. But it is done through human activity, which God has authorized and in which God is known to be present. Thus it is commonly agreed that Genesis 1:1–2:4a is a liturgical text in which the community "remembers" God's creating event, but also reenacts and participates in it in order to give pattern to present experience, presumably in the exile. Praise is not a response to a world already fixed and settled, but it is a responsive and obedient participation in a world that is in the process of being decreed through this liturgical act.

World-Making as an Imaginative Enterprise

An important epistemological shift has happened in our generation[11] in scholarly investigation generally, in Scripture study from *historical* to *literary*,[12] and from the valuing of *facticity* to the celebration of *imagination*. These shifts are all of a piece. They reflect the failure and loss of confidence in Enlightenment modes of knowledge, which were aimed at technical control. We are coming to see that conventional modes of historical-critical investigation—our excessive preoccupation with facticity—are congenial and subservient to an Enlightenment notion of reality that assumes that the world is a fixed, settled object that can be described, analyzed, and finally controlled in an objective way. This objective settlement of reality has left very little for us to do, except to get it right. And we have been able to assume there was a way to get it right.

It has become increasingly clear, however, that reality is not fixed and settled, that it cannot be described objectively. We do not simply respond to a world that is here, but we engage in constituting that world by our participation, our actions, and our speech. As participants in the constitutive act, we do not describe what is there, but we evoke what is not fully there until we act or speak. The human agent, then, is a constitutive part of the enterprise, which means that the shape of reality in part awaits our shaping adherence.

Such a discernment moves our understanding of reality away from a settled absoluteness. That, to be sure, is an awareness that theologians have affirmed for a long time, arguing that God continues to create the world.[13] This affirmation of the dynamic character of creation asserts

- that God is still operative and exercises choices along the way;
- that the world is still open, and we are not fated;
- that human agents, as creatures in God's image, share in God's imaging activity.[14]

I can identify four facets of recent intellectual reflection that illuminate the proposal that praise is constitutive and not merely responsive.

Sociological Understandings

The social world we inhabit is not an inevitable arrangement. It is a chosen or contrived arrangement according to someone's initiative and/or interests. This social world could therefore be arranged differently, if different choices were made according to other initiatives and interests. The most accessible reading of this notion is by Peter L. Berger and Thomas Luckmann, in their illuminating phrase, "the social construction of reality."[15] All three terms of the formulation are important. "Reality" refers to the structure, system, and arrangement of social life that is known, perceived, relied upon, and judged to be true. Reality is everyday life, which is always experienced as "prearranged in patterns."[16] It is the patterning of order that is definitional for daily life.

The second term, "construction," indicates that this pattern or ordering is constructed. It is not a given. The fact that it is not a given is evidenced in the harsh conflict that arises over the rearrangement of patterns of life and power, and the rearrangement of the symbols that legitimate those patterns. Berger and Luckmann say it tersely: "man produces himself."[17] This patterning is not simply "there," as is evidenced by the fact that the lifeworld is patterned differently in different societies. It is chosen, guarded, justified, defended, maintained, at least partly, with intentionality. While a society can greatly prize a certain ordering of experience, the world never needs to be ordered the way it is. It could be ordered differently, or the ordering could be abandoned in disorder that undermines composed relationality.

The third term is "social." Human "self-production" is always and of necessity a social enterprise of the community.[18] Human agents together purpose a human environment. Thus the formula means that the legitimation and patterning of experience, which is daily experienced as reality, is produced and arranged in active ways by the society itself. This special operation is mediated to and appropriated by individuals who live in that society and regard that constructed world as a given.

The process of "world-building" requires that society assert its world as authoritative, accepted as a given without a doubt or reservation, and without any entertainment of a plausible alternative. That process of world construction, as Berger has said so well, depends on adequate and trusting appropriation. On the one hand, there must be externalization, so that the ordering is perceived in the community as objectively true. On the other hand, there must be internalization, so that individuals receive this ordering of experience as "mine." When this reality is accepted as objectively true and personally mine, it becomes a norm (*nomos*) by which all else is tested.

Sociologically, this process of social construction is not simply a response to a world already given. Rather, it is constitutive of a world that is now and always being constructed. Those who sponsor the constructive act regard that constructed world as given. Nonetheless, much energy is put into the construction, especially by those who want it experienced as given.

Thus Berger and Luckmann, I suggest, use the notion of "world" in the same way as Mowinckel.[19] By speaking of world-construction and world-maintenance—that is, active intentional processes of legitimation—Berger and Luckmann are very close to Mowinckel's understanding of cult. Indeed, Berger mentions worship in relation to legitimation.[20] Insofar as Berger is correct, notice that he does not urge that this process ought to be so, but observes that it inevitably is so. Mowinckel's understanding of the Psalms, and of praise, is a specific case in point of Berger's general argument. Israel's hymnic worship is an act of world-construction.

Literary Understandings

A second dimension of human activity that is constitutive of reality is reflected in the current interest in narrative particularly, and in literature more generally.[21] The shift from history to literature in Scripture method, now documented and embraced by a host of scholars, is pertinent to our theme. Focus on historical questions served positivistic notions of reality in which we could recover what was really there as an objective, given reality that only awaited description.

The shift to literary analysis is related to the abandonment of this historical pursuit of objectivity. It is clear that literature not only reports or describes reality, but good literature that is imaginative mediates and redescribes reality. In such literature, the reality that is carried in this particular form did not exist until it was articulated and rendered in exactly this way. That is, speech leads reality, and until reality is spoken, we did not know reality, perceive it, or embrace it. This capacity to lead reality to where it has not yet been is of course the basis of preaching in a sound theology of the Word. Imaginative speech not only describes but constitutes reality.

What Berger and Luckmann present in sociological categories, biblical critics have seen in the literary process. The social community constitutes reality by its authoritative restatement of consensual language. The normative literature mediates a world that would not be available or embraced as a basis for action unless mediated by this literature. Both these sociological and literary approaches take up the central themes of Mowinckel. The social community does not respond to a world that is there, but it awaits a world now to be given, and it constitutes that world through its speech and actions. The literature does not simply comment on a world that is there. It generates a world that would not be there apart from the work and words of the literature. This "world" refers to a set of social relations, perceptions, and gestures that bring order, sequence, and sense to the flux of lived experience. Those social relations, perceptions, and gestures fashion a stable and reliable habitat for humanity.

Psychological Understandings

Recently, the constitutive act of the human agent has been important for personality theory and the psychological disciplines. The awareness that the human person is not a given, but is an ongoing work of freedom, at least to some extent, is found in various theories of personality formation. The human person is an agent who in some part decides and chooses who she or he will be. That person makes those choices in the midst of a community that, along with the person, makes choices, and legitimates or precludes some choices the person may make.

Robert Kegan argues at length that the individual is an active meaning-maker:

> Before long the reader will find the expression "meaning-making organism" redundant; what an organism does, as William Perry says (1970), is organize; and what a human organism organizes is meaning. Thus it is not that a person makes meaning, as much as that the activity of being a person is the activity of meaning-making.[22]

A second theorist contributing to this dynamic understanding of world-making, with a more intentional psychoanalytic frame of reference, is Roy Schafer.[23] In his book *Language and Insight*, Schafer understands linguistic transactions with the therapist as a moment of speech and listening when reality is being constituted, not simply as a report on reality. The two terms—"language" and "insight"—are crucial for Schafer, because he asserts that each fresh linguistic act gives new meaning, shape, and organization to the disturbing and distinctive present. Schafer then suggests that the goal of the therapeutic transaction is to permit the client to participate actively in the process of world-making:

> Thus, when psychoanalysts speak of insight, they necessarily imply emotionally experienced transformation of the analysand, not only as life-history and present world, but as life-historian and world-maker. It is the analysand's transformation and not his or her intellectual recitation of explanations that demonstrates the attainment of useful insight. The analysand has gained a past history and present world that are more intelligible and tolerable

than before, even if still not very enjoyable or tranquil. The past and present are considerably more extensive, cohesive, consistent, humane, and convincingly felt than they were before. But these gains are based as much on knowing *how* as on knowing *that*. Insight is as much a way of looking as it is of seeing anything in particular.[24]

I understand Schafer to mean that the analyst, in their role as interpreter, is to help the person understand the constitutive power of the conversation. It is for this reason that a therapeutic conversation can be transformative, because the speech-event constitutes a new person in a new world that did not exist until or apart from that linguistic transaction. The person helps create themselves in these moments of speech.

A third theorist to mention is Paul Pruyser, who has been particularly attentive to the work of pastors.[25] His study of play and playfulness, in his book entitled *The Play of Imagination*, suggests that the playful, imaginative, illusionary function of the person is an act of hope concerning who the person may yet become and what the world may yet be.

Pruyser begins from a basic psychoanalytic duality between the autistic and the realistic worlds. The autistic world is turned inward in unmitigated desire. The realistic world is one of social demand that requires renunciation. Pruyser concludes, however, that there must also be an illusionistic world, which he correlates and contrasts with the other two worlds. This illusionistic world is an alternative to the other two and the coercive assumption that one must choose between the two. This third world is marked by these phrases: "tutored fantasy," "adventurous thinking," "orderly imagination," "inspired connections," "verbalizable images," and "transcendent objects."[26]

The remainder of Pruyser's book characterizes the process of living in this third world, which he calls "illusion processing," by which he means tutored, disciplined, public imagination. He then reviews how this process is operative in the visual arts, literature, science, religion, and music. In his chapter on religion, he makes some remarkable suggestions about how crucial the play of religion is for society.

All three—Kegan, Schafer, and Pruyser—reflect on the world of creative possibility that in the life of the individual is as yet unfinished. Kegan speaks of "meaning-making," Schafer of "world-making," and Pruyser of "the illusional process." In the moment of speech and imagination, the person evokes, embraces, and experiences a new world.

The three agree

- that the human person is not a given, but an unfinished task;
- that the human person is not fated, but has options and exercises freedom;
- that the exercise of freedom is a constitutive act whereby the person becomes who he or she was not;
- that the essential work of the person is to organize experience in alternative ways;
- that reorganized reality is the person's "world," which shapes, authorizes, and requires actions and possibilities; and
- that this reorganization is creative of a world that happens through speech.

It is clear that these psychological categories of understanding are remarkably congruent with Mowinckel, only cast in personal and interpersonal terms that ignore the possibilities belonging to public (liturgic) acts of constitution.

Theological Understandings

The fourth and final dimension of the constitutive act of "world-making" in current intellectual reflection is the fresh understanding of theology presented by Gordon Kaufman. Kaufman has concluded (more firmly than perhaps most of us) that the old categories of theology have lost their power to evoke and mediate faith.[27] Responsible theology must therefore be a constitutive act, in which our discernment of God must be reconstituted in new ways.

The language Kaufman uses is not without problems. He clearly intends to come very close to the language of the "reconstitution of God" through theological articulation. Taken ontologically, that is obviously a hazardous claim. Taken practically and dramatically, which is in fact how theology is done, each theological articulation intends to render God in a more faithful and more available way.[28] So far as the church is concerned, each such rendering of God offers to the church a "new God" who must be reckoned with in new terms. Clearly the new God in theology that is faithful and disciplined is congruent with the God known in our memory. Yet new speech about God done in the theology and proclamation of the church is never only reiterative, but constructive in some sense for the faith of the church.

The other methodological urging of Kaufman is a distinction between the "real referent," the holy God in actuality who is always unknown and unavailable, and the "available referent," our imaginative construct of God. Since the real referent, in the very nature of God, is unavailable, the available referent is always imaginative and always a construct.[29]

It is my judgment that Kaufman is not as radical as his introductory rhetoric suggests,[30] but he is honest in characterizing what we do in theology. We do in fact, by our words, reconstruct the religious reality that we seek to praise and obey. If one were to say it less radically than Kaufman, we might only say that we continue the ongoing construction of the tradition. Whether one says it in Kaufman's radical rhetoric or in more conventional language, over time the speech of the church shapes the world of faith in which we live. I do not for a moment suggest that such speech-construction finally reshapes the ontology of God, but that it decisively shapes the lifeworld in which we encounter God. Kaufman's intent is to reshape the lifeworld in which we live so that our rhetoric and response may become more commensurate with the extreme dangers that we face—he was primarily concerned with nuclear threat, to which we can add other global crises such as ecological devastation from the effects of climate change, late capitalism, and more.

I have cited four lines of intellectual investigation that reflect the intellectual mood of our post-Enlightenment, postpositivistic situation:

- sociological understandings of the ways in which a community constructs its lifeworld
- literary understandings, which suggest that good literature creates alternative worlds of imagination to provide a home in which we may live and act differently
- psychological understandings of human personality, which suggest that the individual person is an active agent in choosing self

- theological understanding, which suggests that the religious world in which we live is an imaginative construct that mediates our common life

The tendency of all of these approaches is to insist and assume that the "world" in which we live is not a flat, frozen given, but is a particular formation of reality that is established on the basis of trusted speech and gesture. That speech and gesture impose a certain pattern, shape, and legitimacy on our shared experience that could have been patterned, shaped, and legitimated in other ways. Because of the choices that are made in world-construction, however, it *is* this way and not another in this community.

It is the act of praise—the corporate, regularized, intentional, verbalized, and enacted act of praise—through which the community of faith creates, orders, shapes, imagines, and patterns the world of God, the world of faith, the world of life, in which we are to act in joy and obedience. I do not resist the traditional theological claim that praise is response to the God that is already there. But dramatically, liturgically, functionally, the world is as it is when we give it authorized speech. The act of praise is indeed world-making for the community that takes the act of worship as serious and realistic.

Conclusion

My review of four intellectual explorations in various disciplines permits a recovery of Mowinckel's basic insight. From these explorations, I draw three conclusions.

1. Mowinckel is essentially correct to assert that, at a dramatic level, the act of worship does *create a world*. On one hand, we are not so naive as to imagine that there is no world there until the moment of praise. That already-existing world is either disordered and without shape, meaning, and relationality; or, more likely, it is a world that has already been created by some other liturgy so that it has some other shape, meaning, and relationality. To say that there is a world already there is congruent with what the Bible says of creation. The main tendency of the Old Testament is to say

that creation is not "out of nothing" (ex nihilo) (Gen. 1:2), but is an act wrought on chaos that is there—"formless and void" (*tohu wabohu*), not yet a world.[31]

On the other hand, experientially, we may say that the world created by the community is the only world that is there, that is available for me and to which I may gladly and trustingly respond. Sociologically, the lifeworld of my community is the only world that I credit. Literarily, when I am addressed by a good piece of literature, I am required and permitted to suspend all other worlds and commit myself to this world alone. That is the prerequisite of all serious literature. Psychologically, the self I present and construct is the only self I know. The counselor may already perceive another self for me, but that perception is fundamentally irrelevant to me, so long as I am an occupant of this self. That is, the created, constructed world that I inhabit is the only real world, and therefore the task of world-formation is a life-or-death matter.

There are other modes of world-creation in which we participate and to which we are subject. They include advertising, ideology, propaganda, education, and child-nurture. For the community gathered around Jesus, however, it is precisely the act of worship that is the act of world-formation!

2. It is clear, as Amos Wilder has seen, that the lifeworld created in biblical worship is one among many theoretical worlds, and therefore such worship is not only constitutive, but inevitably polemical.[32] Praise insists not only that this is the true world, but that other worlds are false. World-creation also includes world-delegitimation of other worlds. The church sings praises not only toward God but also against the gods.

That polemical function is easily discerned, for example, in hermeneutical quarrels about the use of traditional language and its interface with and impingement upon public and political reality. These interpretive quarrels may not be expressed explicitly. The response to polemical world-making is more likely to be expressed in anger at the door of the church after the service, "I don't see why the church does not stay with religion and out of politics and economics." This response means that the world-construction of the gospel-oriented community has begun to delegitimate other worlds that we had thought to be compatible with or existing alongside this world. When our other worlds are threatened, it evokes resistance and hostility.

More obviously, the quarrels about sexist and feminist or inclusive language are not arguments about language. They are arguments about the world that is there, about the world we shall inhabit, about the ordering of experience that we take as real, reliable, and normative. It is clear that words matter enormously, for words give us worlds in which to live. The particular words of this tradition are crucial, as is attested by both the zeal for new inclusive language and the zeal for conventional language.[33] By the use of our words we construct worlds! It is clear that the words with which we praise God shape the world of legitimacy in which we live.

3. Finally, the agent who fashions the liturgy is a key agent in the process of world-construction. In her book on professional ethics, Karen Lebacqz has discerningly characterized the power entrusted to professionals. More precisely about the minister as a professional, Lebacqz asserts:

> The minister does not simply heal or help or console. She defines reality by offering a new language, a perspective on hidden meanings, a transformation of ordinary symbols, a hope in the midst of seeming hopelessness. . . . The social construction of reality is at the heart of the minister's vocation.[34]

Lebacqz's account, rooted in a sociology of symbols, is surely correct. It is correct, moreover, for ministers who may not recognize their powerful function and who may do this work without self-awareness or intentionality. Lebacqz's insight from sociology is reenforced and deepened by our theological awareness of the ministerial office. It is precisely the task of ministry to convene, evoke, form, and re-form a community of praise and obedience.

Every aspect of a pastor's work is aimed at this function of ministry. But the pastor's work happens in the context of and as a function of the "work of the whole church," which we call liturgy. In its liturgical life the church, led by the Spirit, engages in praise and obedience and so constitutes and is constituted as God's people. Thus, the intellectual developments that I have explored in this chapter help us to see what in fact is underway theologically and liturgically in the church. What is underway is the formation of an alternative community. This work of the church is of course in response to the command of God and is indeed human work. It is at the same time, however, in inscrutable and undeniable ways, a moment when the voice of God is enacted "who gives life to the dead and calls into existence the things that do not exist" (Rom. 4:17).

Questions for Reflection

1. Brueggemann considers the act of worship as a "constitutive act" that not only responds to but also, by God's design, helps create the world in which participants live. In what ways have you experienced praise and worship as a world-making act? What elements of worship illumine that idea for you?

2. What are some problematic social constructions you recognize operating in the systems and structures of our shared reality today? (Consider constructs of race, class, sexuality, family, economics, politics, etc.) What role does the worship of God play in helping imagine alternatives to those constructs as God's world continues to be created?

3. How have you experienced the constitutive power of world-making in literary or psychological arenas? What memorable literary worlds have you entered into? Has talking about the self in a psychological context ever helped create a new reality for you? What insights do these examples give you about how "in the moment of speech and imagination, the person evokes, embraces, and experiences a new world" (p. 34)?

4. How do you understand the responsibility of pastors or worship leaders for world-making as they craft language for praise and worship? What world is being created in your community of faith through the words used in worship?

Chapter 3

The Counterworld of the Psalms

Two Questions about the Psalms and One Answer

First, why is it that the Psalms hold such a compelling place in our faith, our worship, and our spirituality? Why is it that in liturgical churches we get a psalm every Sunday, or at least a snippet of a psalm? How is it that this old poetry continues to occupy us and to generate an endless literature, sometimes scholarly, but more often popular and devotional?

The second question flies in the face of the first: Why is it, given this excessive preoccupation with the Psalms, that we mostly know only a handful of them? Beyond "The LORD is my shepherd" in Psalm 23, we know, "I lift up my eyes to the hills" in Psalm 121, "God is our refuge and strength" in Psalm 46, and perhaps a few others—or, rather, *snippets* of a few others, to be precise. Even liturgical churches manage very often to exclude and disregard psalms that do not fit with what has become the happy, reassuring mode of gospel faith in our therapeutic culture. Even with the psalms we use, it has become mandatory to edit out the objectionable parts. I have had opportunity to observe even the most faithful who cannot tolerate all the verses in Psalm 109 with its thirst for vengeance. So it is that we find parts of the Psalms problematic, at least, and often so scandalous that they must be dismissed.

These, then, are my two opening questions: (1) Why do we cling to the Psalter? (2) Why do we so aggressively limit the parts of the Psalter to which we cling? Or, put differently: why do we have a love-hate relationship with the Psalms? Why are we so ambivalent about this script of faith?

41

I suggest that one answer will suffice for both questions. Because we have a closely held world of sign, symbol, and memory (often unnamed, unacknowledged, and certainly uncriticized) that pertains to every part of our life, we know that the Psalms voice and mediate to us a counterworld that is at least in tension with, and in fact is often also directly opposed to, our other, closely held world. As a result, we yearn for a new, improved world that is occupied by the Good Shepherd, that yields help from the hills, and that attests a reliable refuge and strength. That is why we continually line out these particular cadences again and again. That is why we want to hear them at the hospital, the graveside, and in the many venues where our closely held world is known to be thin and inadequate. We want something more and something other than what our closely held world can possibly yield.

But that same answer is also a response to the question concerning why we avoid so much of the Psalter. It is because we recognize intuitively that the counterworld of the Psalms is a risky, raw-edged world of dispute and contestation, and that is often more than we can take on. The God whom we meet in the Psalms is not the benign object of custodial religion in which we specialize, but is a Character, Agent, and Force who operates in free ways that disturb and interrupt. Thus I suggest that we are both drawn to and flee from the Psalms, at one and the same time. We want that counterworld offered there to us, but we dread its performance, which challenges our closely held world in so many and so compelling ways.

Thus I propose that every time the church lines out a psalm and every time the pastor preaches from the Psalter, we are performing, yet again, a counterworld that we welcome and that we dread. In what follows I will first describe, as best I can, the closely held world we inhabit and that we bring with us when we come to church. I will then describe the counterworld scripted for us in the Psalms that invites our "reperformance" (see chap. 1).

Our Closely Held World

The world we carry with us has shaped us and continues to shape us. It remains largely unrecognized and uncriticized, but it is a product of powerful, often intentional nurture, inculcation, instruction, and propaganda. It is a world imposed on us but which we, in many ways, have ourselves internalized. There is no doubt that this world is taken up differently by each of us, depending on our particular narrative past, present circumstance, and current company of companions. Here I will speak in summary fashion about our closely held world, such that one may have to add or take away from it, depending on how much of it rings true. In any event, I will identify seven marks of the dominant ideology of our culture that I believe pertain to our commonly assumed, unnamed world. There is more to be said about this world than I can say here, but I will nevertheless identify some dark elements that I think are in tension with the counterworld of the Psalter.

Anxiety and Scarcity

First, our closely held world is a world of *anxiety* that is rooted in *scarcity*. It is a world that is worried about running out, not having enough, not having done enough, not having been enough, not measuring up, not being safe, valued, or esteemed. I think, moreover, that it is part of the policy and intention of the present powers to keep us anxious, because those deep in anxiety are more likely to conform.

Beyond that, the advertising liturgies of capitalism on TV constantly remind us that we have not yet arrived, that we do not yet have the right product that will make us safe, prosperous, and happy. The unspoken message is that we are currently unsafe, unprosperous, and unhappy, and we will continue to be so until we "buy in." It is surely the case that anxiety is to some extent an inescapable human condition, but to dub ours as "the age of anxiety" is to acknowledge that ours is acutely so, and to some extent that acute anxiety is ideologically produced in an intentional way. As a result, we travel with a constant eye on scarcity, and consequently, we ration. We ration health care and food. But we also ration grace, limiting those who may have access to our "goodies," whether immigrants who want a safe home, or women who want to be ordained, or gays who want to be married. We worry that if the goodies and power are shared more widely, there will not be as much for us. Indeed, there will not be enough!

Greed

Second, our closely held world of anxiety rooted in scarcity evokes an ideology of *greed*. The mantra for that social reality comes from Gordon Gekko's line in the 1987 film *Wall Street*: "Greed is good." The outcome is a rapacious world in which those who can get do so; those who have get more, and for such greedy appetites, there is then need for cheap labor and the wounding of those who are not fast enough or positioned well enough for the rat race. Greed becomes the force to break up neighborly relations and to transform those relationships into contest, dispute, and conflict. The ideology of anxious scarcity generates artificial needs, so that unthinkable luxuries are quickly redefined as necessities. That greed then requires fatiguing overwork, endless 24/7 electronic connection, and insatiable multitasking, all in an effort to get ahead, or stay even, and not to fall hopelessly behind. Such an embrace of greed initiates an endless process, because capitalism is insanely predicated on infinite expansion, and limitless desire is never satisfied.

Self-Sufficiency

Third, the drive of anxiety that propels greed leads to a notion of *self-sufficiency*, either the winsome notion that I *can be* self-sufficient and can make it on my own, or the dread recognition that I *must be* self-sufficient, as others are all rivals and competitors. The lure of self-sufficiency is signaled already by Pharaoh, who could shamelessly declare:

> My Nile is my own;
> I made it for myself.
> Ezek. 29:3

The claim resounds in the man in the parable who could boast in self-satisfaction:

> I will do this: I will pull down my barns and build larger ones, and there I will store all my grain and my goods. And I will say to my soul, Soul, you have ample goods laid up for many years; relax, eat, drink, be merry. (Luke 12:18–19)

Recently, I was in an academic context in which a sociologist championed self-sufficiency. He dared to say about winter-produced tomatoes: "They are man-made. There is no mystery in the process. They are designed and grown and distributed solely by human effort." I am sorry that I did not have the wits at the time to say, "That must be why they taste so bad." We are, here and now, only a belated version of Israel, who was sorely tempted to boast in the new land:

> When you have eaten your fill and have built fine houses and live in them, and when your herds and flocks have multiplied, and your silver and gold is multiplied, and all that you have is multiplied, then do not exalt yourself. . . . Do not say to yourself, "My power and the might of my own hand have gotten me this wealth." (Deut. 8:12–14, 17)

For good or for ill, our world is "without God," for God is at best an ancient superstition who makes no sense in the speedy world of contemporary control.

Denial

Fourth, our closely held world of endless competitiveness is a system that cannot keep its promises of safety, prosperity, and happiness; it does not fully work. And so we are seduced into *denial* about the dysfunction of our dominant defining system of public life. We are forced into denial because we must pretend that the system works for us, that we have mastered the system, and that we benefit from it. We must keep up appearances, even if only to match the Joneses, who are also keeping up appearances. We are on our best behavior, constantly expressing confidence in the system, rendering service to the system, and imagining that if we do a little bit better, it will be in our favor.

But of course beneath the surface of such pretense, we know better. We know that a new car will not make us super. We know that a different beer will not surround us with friends we can trust or in whom we can confide, and so no one ever talks to anyone in a beer ad—not in any depth, at any rate. We know that a better shave will not get us a lover. We know that more weapons will not bring us safety. We know that wars do not produce as many "haves" as they produce displaced persons. We know that the violence in football is a mighty narcotic for us, but never about anything more than the "bread and circuses" of virility, money, and power. We know that the so-called political dialogue is ultimately about controlling the wealth for the ones who manage the process.

We know all of that, but we must collude. Because if we are not team players, we will not be "friended," and we will drop out; consequently, we bury the hurt-filled truth that will surface at night when we are alone and our defenses are down . . . or that will surface in random acts of violence that are to be predicted but are always unexpected. We collude, after a restless night of candor, for the sake of the next day, whenever (which is to say, *always*) we reengage the performance of the system yet again one more time, despite our gnawing awareness.

Despair

But because we cannot fully master and sustain such denial and from time to time gasp before the truth that our world is not working, we end in *despair*. There are lots of healthy, honest reasons for despair at present, because the old world some of us have loved as white, tenured males is now gone. The church at the center of the village will never come back. The "Greatest Generation" now yields to a generation of self-occupied, narcissistic people, and it becomes harder and harder to care much about the common good. We have this sinking feeling about the prospect of a funded retirement, and now we not only lock all the doors but even cower behind them. We know enough to know that something strange has happened to our environment and our health, whatever we may openly or officially admit. We sense our world in free fall and doubt that there is any bottom to it. We become short-tempered, inhospitable, and uncaring, no longer having reason to care or any expectation that our caring will matter. We are sapped of energy and left alone in our woefulness, not believing in any possible hope of repair.

Amnesia

It is all too much. And as a result, we are all too happy to press the delete button labeled *amnesia*:

"If only I could blank all of that out. I can live now, in this moment, in the world immediately in front of me. There is so much I cannot afford to remember about misjudgment and exhibits of my dark side, and the dark side of our common life, of My Lai, Auschwitz, Hiroshima, and the common legacy of slavery. I do not want to know anymore about the atrocities committed by my government on my behalf. I do not want to think anymore about the fraud of food and drug labeling and the ways that big money works invisibly to shape my life. I do not want to worry anymore about the scars of slavery and the burns of napalm. I do not want to be reminded of the ovens of Poland or the walls in Israel or Arizona. I do not want to know how many gay people there are, or how many young women are sold every day into sex slavery. I do not want to hear about the violence in our prisons. I just want to sing songs of joy and happiness—praise songs that have no narrative to remind us of anything beyond this particular moment of pious goodwill and non-memory."

Sometimes we prefer "don't ask, don't tell" amnesia. "Don't tell me, and I will not ask, and I will get through the day in my isolated innocence." But Moses said over and over, "Take heed lest you forget." But we *do* want to forget and not bear the hurt of all the misadventure that continues in our common life. It is enough to be here and now in my family and my little tribe, gladly disconnected from all else.

A Normless World

Seventh, the outcome of our narcissistic amnesia is a *normless world*, because without God, without tradition, and without common good, everything is possible. We have arrived at an out-of-control foreign policy that takes torture to be acceptable. We have watched the disappearance of civic courtesy and the emergence of crudeness, shrillness, and road rage that are emblems of the new privatism. Without God, our life has only (and at best) a private meaning. Without God, might makes right, so we must acquire all the muscle we can.

But the ultimate outcome of this normless world is that I am left alone and at risk. When they come for me, there will be no one to speak up for me, no one to help—because I never spoke up and never helped out either.

Perhaps this picture of our closely held world is too dark—maybe even more than should be said. I am aware that there are important islands of generosity and oceans of healthy venues; I do not wish to minimize these gestures and actions to the contrary. But my conviction is that the ideological, systemic force of our dominant world has generated a context that is antihuman in its assumptions, practices, and futures. It is almost more than can be borne, because this ideological, systemic force is so relentless and so pervasive that it overwhelms us more often than not, leaving us exceedingly vulnerable.

The Counterworld of the Psalms

These dark markings of our closely held world are countered by the resolved speech and imagination of the Psalms. We long for this counterworld, and so we are drawn to the Psalms, which give us cadences of another language with another reference that we hear and recite and sing and sense. But when we encounter the Psalms, we find its counterworld deeply subversive, and so we fear that our closely held world will be exposed or undermined. We enter into the Psalter with deep ambiguity: partly eager for alternative, partly in dread of alternative. The counterworld in the Psalms is thus fraught with significance. A great deal is at stake in the voicing of this counterworld. In what follows, I focus on a particular psalm for each of seven markings of the counterworld of the Psalms, but ultimately I am working with psalmic genres, not simply specific examples, so that the claim of one psalm may be extended to many others.

Trustful Fidelity

The counterworld of the Psalms contradicts our world of anxiety by mediating to us a world of *trustful fidelity*. The book of Psalms is voiced in the midst of immense threat. It evidences a world under threats that go by many names, all the way from cosmic chaos to historical enemies to ominous "evildoers" who may have magical powers. The Psalms know all about threat—these specific threats and threat in general.

But that threat is contradicted by the world over which YHWH presides in reliable fidelity. The anxiety of the world is contradicted by the transformative attentiveness of God. Psalm 27 moves back and forth between acknowledged threat and glad submission to a decisive affirmation of God. First, the threat is named: evildoers who assail, adversaries and foes (v. 2); an encamped army (v. 3); enemies (v. 6); false witnesses (v. 12).

The poet gives full voice to the threat. But the threat is countered by the reality of God:

> The LORD is my light and my salvation;
>> whom shall I fear?
> The LORD is the stronghold of my life;
>> of whom shall I be afraid?
>>>> v. 1

> For he will hide me in his shelter
>> in the day of trouble;
> he will conceal me under the cover of his tent;
>> he will set me high on a rock.
>>>> v. 5

Verses 1–4 are a statement of confidence. What follows after that is a plea that the God whom the psalmist trusts act yet again. We get a series of imperatives that are uttered in confidence:

> Hear,
> Be gracious. (v. 7)
> Do not hide,
> Do not turn me away,
> Do not cast me off. (v. 9)
> Do not give me up. (v. 12)

The psalm pivots on the word "though," which is an act of defiance. It is a bold and brave "nevertheless, notwithstanding":

> *Though* war rise up against me,
>> yet I will be confident.
>>> v. 3b

This "though" of resolve has echoes elsewhere:

> Therefore we will not fear,
>> *though* the earth should change,
>> *though* the mountains shake in the heart of the sea;
>> *though* its waters roar and foam,
>> *though* the mountains tremble with its tumult.
>>> 46:2–3

> *Though* the fig tree does not blossom,
>> and no fruit is on the vines;
> *though* the produce of the olive fails,
>> and the fields yield no food;
> *though* the flock is cut off from the fold,
>> and there is no herd in the stalls,
> yet I will rejoice in the LORD;
> I will exult in the God of my salvation.
>> Hab. 3:17–18

This "though" is a well-grounded, adamant refusal to participate in the anxiety that is all around.

A World of Abundance

The counterworld of the Psalms contradicts our world of greed by mediating to us a *world of abundance* in which greed is completely inappropriate. The ground for such an abundance that refuses greed is the glad doxological affirmation that God is the creator who has blessed and funded the earth so that it is a gift that keeps on giving. The doxological assumption is that when God's creatures practice justice, God's earth responds with new gifts. Our anxiety that funds greed is undone by abundance that funds grateful generosity. That divine generosity is not determined by quantities or possessions, but by a panoply of gifts that defy quantification. The doxological attitude of the Psalms makes grasping for more unnecessary, so that the compulsion for usurpation is nullified in doxological practice. One might consider any of the great creation doxologies, but Psalm 145 is an excellent case study in the alternative to greed. The psalm begins with a catalog of divine acts that are inexplicable but not doubted in the poetry. In sequence the language of divine miracle goes like this: works, mighty acts, majesty, wondrous works, awesome deeds, greatness, abundant goodness, righteousness. These terms are all rough synonyms that attest to the way that God overwhelms the world with goodness.

Beginning in verse 13, in celebration of the rule of YHWH, we get a barrage of rhetoric that gives accent to "all":

> The LORD is faithful in *all* his words,
>   and gracious in *all* his deeds.
> The LORD upholds *all* who are falling,
>   and raises up *all* who are bowed down.
> The eyes of *all* look to you,
>   and you give them their food in due season.
> You open your hand,
>   satisfying the desire of *every* living thing.
> The LORD is just in *all* his ways,
>   and kind in *all* his doings.
> The LORD is near to *all* who call on him,
>   to *all* who call on him in truth.
> He fulfills the desire of *all* who fear him;
>   he also hears their cry, and saves them.
> The LORD watches over *all* who love him.
> Ps. 145:13–20

The image is an overflow of limitless blessing given without reservation to all who are in need and turn to the creator. The much-used table prayer in verses 15–16 is an act of defiance against any temptation to greed. We eat because it is a gift. Food is given as a gift. It is not an achievement or an accomplishment or a possession. When creation is recognized as a gift that keeps giving so that loaves abound, we need not covet what is on the plate of our neighbor. We need not hoard. We need not acquire a surplus because we may run out, because this is the God who gives far more abundantly than we can ask or imagine.

I should be honest enough to notice that there is one more "all" in Psalm 145, a quite curious note in context in verse 20: "but *all* the wicked he will destroy." The term *wicked* is generic and lacks specificity. In context, however, it might well be taken precisely as a reference to those who are greedy, who do not trust the divine abundance, and who thereby skew the neighborhood, confiscating food that belongs to others, and who do all that because of anxiety about scarcity. The overflow of poetic doxology is a verbal counter-point for the overflow of gift from God, so that word matches divine gesture. The psalm verbally matches the sacrament of creation. The outpouring of doxological language is commensurate with the out-pouring of the gifts of creation.

Ultimate Dependence

The counterworld of the Psalms contradicts our closely held world of self-sufficiency by mediating to us a world confident in God's preferential option for those who call on him in their *ultimate dependence*. Psalm 10 amounts almost to a field analysis of social power. The psalm knows of the self-sufficient who acknowledge no limit or accountability. They are arrogant in their use of other people for their own self-enhancement. They dismiss God as a bad idea:

> For the wicked boast of the desires of their heart,
>   those greedy for gain curse and renounce the LORD.
> In the pride of their countenance the wicked say,
>   "God will not seek it out";
>   all their thoughts are, "There is no God.". . .
> They think in their heart, "We shall not be moved;
>   throughout all generations we shall not meet adversity.". . .
> They think in their heart, "God has forgotten,
>   he has hidden his face, he will never see it."
>
> 10:3–4, 6, 11

At the same time, they prey on and devour the poor:

> they lurk in secret like a lion in its covert;
> they lurk that they may seize the poor;
>   they seize the poor and drag them off in their net.
>
> v. 9

The two always go together: get rid of God, and you can get rid of the neighbor as well.

The psalm celebrates the voice of the vulnerable who, by their prayers, not only assert trust and dependence on God, but also estab-lish a working alliance with God, who is recruited into the cause of the vulnerable. Thus self-sufficiency is countered by glad, trusting dependence on God, which issues in bold imperatives:

> Rise up, O LORD; O God, lift up your hand;
> > do not forget the oppressed. . . .
> Break the arm of the wicked and evildoers;
> > seek out their wickedness until you find none.
> > > vv. 12, 15

Thus, the unequal ground between the self-sufficient and their helpless victims is corrected by the entry of YHWH on the side of the vulnerable. In this portrayal of glad reliance on YHWH—and in contrast to the default claim of the settled—rather than reliance on the self, the confident conclusion is that God is committed to the cause of those who cannot help themselves:

> O LORD, you will hear the desire of the meek;
> > you will strengthen their heart, you will incline your ear
> to do justice for the orphan and the oppressed,
> > so that those from earth may strike terror no more.
> > > vv. 17–18

Those who "strike terror" are the *self-sufficient* who believe they are permitted to do whatever they are able to do. But the counterreliance on the God of justice means that such self-sufficiency cannot and will not prevail in the end. These terrorists differ from the terrorists so much in the news. These terrorists operate covertly inside the permits of the law. They are nonetheless agents of violence against the vulnerable.

Abrasive Truth-Telling

The counterworld of the Psalms contradicts our closely held world of denial by mediating to us a world of *abrasive truth-telling*. This is one of the recurring and most surprising elements of the Psalms, one that confounds pious readers. The Psalms refuse denial, insisting that the full truth must be told, most especially the truth of pain that is grounded in infidelity—whether to God or to neighbor. The entire genre of lament, complaint, and protest constitutes a refusal of denial. Incidentally, this is the very same set of Psalms that the church most often and harmfully ignores. The truth-telling of lament is important, not only for the specific truths it tells, but also and even more because of the witness that truth-telling is not only necessary, but permitted—even required! The community of the Psalter is resolved to be a truth-telling community!

Consider Psalm 44, a psalm we rarely if ever use. It is a complaint of Israel in its suffering and abandonment due to a national defeat, likely the sixth-century destruction of Judah and Jerusalem, the 9/11 of the Old Testament. In verses 1–8 the psalm begins with a lavish song of thanks to YHWH for past deliverances that Israel gladly recalls, concluding in this way:

> In God we have boasted continually,
>> and we will give thanks to your name forever.
>>>> 44:8

But then, in an abrupt reversal for which we are not prepared, the psalm turns on YHWH in the present crisis with a series of frontal accusations, the kind that pious folk avoid at all costs. The address to God is a direct "you" that pounds in repetition:

> Yet you have rejected us and abased us,
>> and have not gone out with our armies.
> You made us turn back from the foe,
>> and our enemies have gotten spoil.
> You have made us like sheep for slaughter,
>> and have scattered us among the nations.
> You have sold your people for a trifle,
>> demanding no high price for them.
> You have made us the taunt of our neighbors,
>> the derision and scorn of those around us.
> You have made us a byword among the nations,
>> a laughingstock among the peoples.
>>>> vv. 9–14

After an interlude, the conclusion is reached with a double "yet," the first absolving Israel of any guilt, the second convicting YHWH of infidelity:

> All this has come upon us,
>> *yet* we have not forgotten you,

or been false to your covenant.
Our heart has not turned back,
    nor have our steps departed from your way,
yet you have broken us in the haunt of jackals,
    and covered us with deep darkness.

vv. 17–19

Then follows a vigorous fivefold imperative petition:

Rouse yourself!
Awake,
do not cast us off! (v. 23)
Rise up,
Redeem us. (v. 26)

These expectant imperatives are enmeshed with rhetorical questions that amount to another accusation against God:

Why do you sleep, O Lord? . . .
Why do you hide your face?
    Why do you forget our affliction and oppression?

vv. 23–24

These questions are neither hypothetical nor rhetorical. The three-fold "why" is not a request seeking new information, but a sharp reprimand. The Psalter knows that truth-telling is indispensable for well-being, even if the truth in question somehow scandalizes God. Israel is not afraid to declare out loud that the "system" in God's world is not working. In fact, Israel will abide it no longer!

A World of Hope

The counterworld of the Psalms also contradicts our closely held world by mediating to us a *world of hope*. My case study here is the dialogue of the self found in Psalms 42–43. These psalms (and others) offer a road map of emotional extremity that evokes the many "faces" or selves of the self.

The poet of Psalms 42–43 can remember happy liturgical occasions in the past (42:4), as well as the thunderous waterfalls of the mighty cataracts of Mount Hermon, all of which attest to God's steadfast love (42:6–8). The whole of creation sounds an ongoing song of praise to the creator:

> By day the LORD commands his steadfast love,
>   and at night his song is with me,
>   a prayer to the God of my life.
>
> v. 8

Such memories, however, are only a context for the present reality of despair. In verse 3, the speaker is not able to affirm the steadfast love of "day and night" that will be asserted in verse 8. In verse 3, the memories are vexed venues for tears:

> My tears have been my food
>   day and night,
> while people say to me continually,
>   "Where is your God?"

What people ask the psalmist is what he must ask himself: "Where is God?" More poignantly still: "Where is *my* God? The one who helped me in times past?" Now it is day after day and night after night of divine absence, endless crying, enemies, deadly wounds, and taunting adversaries. The psalmist has ample reason to despair and to question God's faithful attentiveness. The question is not only out in the open, in the neighborhood, so to speak. It is also his private anguish, deep in nights of tears, a wonderment he cannot avoid. Where indeed?

But the poet refuses to give in to the most obvious conclusion to be drawn about God's absence. He refuses to let the circumstance of abandonment and helplessness define him. And so, in the face of such unbearable trouble, he issues a command to God:

> Vindicate me, O God, and defend my cause
>   against an ungodly people;
> From those who are deceitful and unjust
>   deliver me!
> For you are the God in whom I take refuge;
>   why have you cast me off?
> Why must I walk about mournfully
>   because of the oppression of the enemy?

O send out your light and your truth;
   let them lead me;
let them bring me to your holy hill
   and to your dwelling.

43:1–3

The poet anticipates receiving liturgical well-being.

In the midst of all the grieving, the psalm discloses an internal dialogue wherein the voice of the faithful self speaks to the doubting self. The faithful self both poses a question and issues an answer in reply:

Why are you cast down, O my soul,
   and why are you disquieted within me?
Hope in God; for I shall again praise him,
   my help and my God.

42:11

Why are you cast down, O my soul,
   and why are you disquieted within me?
Hope in God; for I shall again praise him,
   my help and my God.

43:5

The issue at hand is about being cast down, bowed down, and defeated. But the psalmist, who is so well situated in the tradition, has resources that enable him to refuse to stay there. The question is posed . . . twice. But the response is vigorous . . . twice: Hope in God! Hope in God! Which is to say: "Do not hope in self. Do not hope in progress. Do not hope for luck." It is exactly the God of fidelity who is the ground of hope. Mobilization of that God, effective human mobilization of that God, is the antidote to despair. The Psalms anticipate the parable of Jesus about the impatient widow (Luke 18:1–8). She is a model of petition before the uncaring judge. Prayer of this vigorous kind is an antidote to losing heart. Our closely held world of despair is a wasteland of abandoned hearts. But Israel knows better in its covenantal life. That is why we gather to lift up our hearts. That is why "you gotta have heart," to tell the truth, to remember, and to anticipate—all acts of self-awareness and belonging. Hope is the great refusal of Israel!

Lively Remembering

The counterworld of the Psalms contradicts our closely held world of amnesia and mediates to us a world of *lively remembering*. Everywhere in the Psalms remembering is a game-changer. Here we can make particular reference to the so-called historical psalms, the ones in which Israel voices its "canonical" inventory of YHWH's faithful, transformative actions. It is clear that the remembering in these psalms is not just "for the record," and surely it is not flat-footed reportage. Rather these psalms' memories characteristically have an immediate, contemporary payoff.

The climax of *Psalm 105*'s long recital of great deeds is, "that they might keep his statutes and observe his laws" (Ps. 105:45). The purpose of remembering is thus to evoke a contemporary practice of obedience in the wake of the memory. The implied negative is that when the inventory of miracles is forgotten, there will be no contemporary obedience (see Ps. 78:5–8). When the tradition is scuttled or neglected, the maintenance of covenantal obedience is put at risk (see Jer. 2:8).

In *Psalm 106*, a companion to Psalm 105, the same inventory is recited, but this time the focus is on the recurring recalcitrance of infidelity on the part of Israel. That is, it is a confession of sin, and it ends in petition:

> Save us, O LORD our God,
>   and gather us from among the nations,
> that we may give thanks to your holy name
>   and glory in your praise.
>
> 106:47

This is the petition of a people scattered among the nations who wait to be gathered home. This prayer anticipates that the current negativity might turn to praise and thanksgiving because of God's transformative action. In both Psalms 105 and 106, then, the bid for obedience and the bid for rescue depend on memory. Without memory, there will be no obedience on the part of Israel and no rescue on the part of God. Indeed, without remembering there is no life with God.

In *Psalm 136*, the whole history is again recited, punctuated this time with the repeated refrain, "for his steadfast love endures forever." All of Israel's history, indeed all of world history, is an arena that exhibits God's abiding fidelity. It would be a useful pastoral exercise, in each of the modes of obedience, rescue, and fidelity, to add verses to these "historical psalms" that bring them to the present day, reciting recent miracles, naming recent recalcitrances, affirming recent fidelities. These recitals connect a past of fidelity and infidelity to the present, where fidelity is in play, and to the future, when anything might happen—all of that within a society that craves forgetting and being disconnected. But, in the main and for the most part, Israel has no delete button when it comes to its complex life with God.

Normed Fidelity

The counterworld of the Psalms contradicts our closely held world of normlessness by mediating to us a world of *normed fidelity*. That normed fidelity is available to us because God has disclosed to Israel, in the form of the Torah, a will and a purpose other than our own, not subject to negotiation. That will and purpose are encoded at Sinai in the Ten Commandments. But since Sinai, Israel has developed a rich corpus of interpretation, a legacy of commentary that resets the old commandments, ever again and always, into new times, places, and circumstances. We are told that Ezra, second only to Moses, "gave interpretation" to the Torah that he had read. And when Israel, after Ezra, used the term "Torah" (never meaning simply or simplistically "law"), it refers to the entire legacy of norming that is elastic, dynamic, fluid, and summoning. The outcome of that legacy in the Psalter is the great Torah Psalms in which Israel celebrates, with joy, that the creator God has not left the world normless, but has instilled in the very structure of creation the transformative capacity for enacted fidelity.

That is why Psalm 19 juxtaposes the glory of creation that attests the creator (Ps. 19:1–6) with the commandments that are the source of life. The poet offers six parallel statements, six outcomes of Torah, six transformative verbs, six great new possibilities:

> The law of the LORD is perfect,
> reviving the soul;

> the decrees of the LORD are sure,
>   making wise the simple;
> the precepts of the LORD are right,
>   rejoicing the heart;
> the commandment of the LORD is clear,
>   enlightening the eyes;
> the fear of the LORD is pure,
>   enduring forever;
> the ordinances of the LORD are true
>   and righteous altogether.
>
> 19:7–9

The product of an obeyed Torah is joy and well-being, as surely as the consequence of normlessness is an unsustainable jungle of power and threat.

It is no wonder, then, that the psalmist can assert that the commandments are better than gold (19:10), because what can gold of itself do for life? It is no wonder that another psalmist can exclaim,

> Oh, how I love your *Torah*!
> Ps. 119:97

> [Y]our *Torah* is my delight
> v. 174

It is the Torah that yields identity and perfect freedom. It is indeed a gift to come down where we ought to be!

To summarize: these seven features of the Psalter's world constitute a transformative alternative to, and severe contradiction of, the world we hold so close, which is the dominant ideology of our culture. No wonder we love the Psalter, because it mediates to us this counterworld in which we may practice fidelity. But it is also no wonder that we resist and redact the Psalter, because it exposes our closely held world as both threat and fraud. Thus I propose that every time we go near a psalm, we are engaging in subversive action. It is a sub-version of the big version of reality to which we have unwittingly succumbed.

The Psalter is not a collection of beautiful sayings from which we can lift pious snippets. It is, taken as a whole, the ground and constitution of an entirely different lifeworld, one that refuses to let us live in the thin world of anxiety, greed, self-sufficiency, denial, despair, amnesia, and normlessness. The Psalter shows us that the dominant world given us in our culture is not the real world, and we need not inhabit it. Instead, we may indeed lift our hearts in joy and enter into another realm—one of weeping and laughing, even if that weeping is now and the laughing only later (Ps. 30:5; Luke 6:21–25).

Questions for Reflection

1. What verses of the Psalms do you know by heart? In what ways do they provide a vision of "a new, improved world that is occupied by the Good Shepherd, that yields help from the hills, and that attests a reliable refuge and strength"? What verses from the Psalms that you know and love are often edited out of personal and communal recitations?

2. Where do you see evidence of the dominant cultural ideologies of anxiety, scarcity, greed, and self-sufficiency at work? How do they manifest in your day-to-day life? What would change if you could resist them to more fully occupy the counterworld of the Psalms?

3. How comfortable are you with the Psalms' example of "abrasive truth-telling" as a required element of a faithful community? What complaint about suffering, or confession of infidelity, have you not ever voiced to God? Alongside this, what statement of hope and remembering of God's transformative action can you summon up to connect past, present, and future instances of God's fidelity, and the call to obedience?

4. Review below the seven features of the counterworld of the Psalms, juxtaposed with our culture's dominant narratives. What verses from the Psalms can you add to your personal canon, to push back on those narratives and keep the Psalter's subversive world in view?

   - anxiety vs. trustful fidelity
   - greed vs. a world of abundance
   - self-sufficiency vs. ultimate dependence
   - denial vs. abrasive truth-telling
   - despair vs. a world of hope
   - amnesia vs. lively remembering
   - normlessness vs. normed fidelity

PART TWO

Praise and Doxology

Chapter 4

Praise and the Psalms

A Politics of Glad Abandonment, Part One

*P*raise is an odd, amorphous theme. Among other things, as seen in previous chapters, it puts us at odds with a technically oriented world, and it plunges us promptly into an ecumenical matrix. The discussion that follows is in three parts: a theoretical statement, an exegetical statement, and a practical statement. My urging is a modest one: that serious parishes and congregations must invest greatly and intentionally as communities of praise, and, indeed, that they have no more important work to do.

First, I shall state eleven theses on the nature of praise. In these theses, I shall regard the church as *humanity in praise, ceding its life over to God.*[1]

1. Praise is *a liturgical act* with its own "reasons of the heart," not submitted to the reasons of this age. That is, praise is a daring departure from all things scientific and rational, and therefore is not available for our conventional explanations and understandings. It is especially odd and scandalous that parishes peopled by the best-educated, the most powerful, and the most affluent and influential should engage in such a prerational act. They bear loud witness to the premise that life does not consist in achievement, control, or objectivity, but that the root realities of our life are prerational and partake of mystery, gift, and amazement. Thus life finally will not be mastered by technique but partakes definitionally of freighted artistry, of mystery that we categorize as sacrament.[2] Liturgy is our fleeting resolve to have done with technique and control as ways of locating sense, meaning, value, and hope in our lives. Liturgy is embrace of an alternative image of reality.

2. Praise is *a poetic act.* That is, the church speaks in large, metaphorical phrasings that are evocative, generative, suggestive, and ultimately constitutive but resist every closed meaning. This poetic act is genuinely polyvalent, that is, open to many meanings and therefore not coercive, and not reductionist, wide in latitude and accepting of versions of reality other than our own. Such praise is willing to grant those who listen to praise (including God) freedom in construing what we assert and claim as a mode of discourse. Thus praise is deeply opposed to memo, even as sacrament opposes technique. Memos reduce, minimize, routinize, and seek to control; this sung poetry leaves things open in respect, awe, and astonishment. If we eventually become the way we talk, if reality sooner or later follows speech, then the utterance of doxology may eventually wean us away from our memo-shaped mastery that resists and resents every ambiguity, because speech without ambiguity has no power to heal or transform.[3] Doxology creates imaginative space in which ambiguity may open to alternative.

3. Praise is *an audacious act.* It is our intentional "outloudness" that breaks the silence and is a risk of self-assertion in the very presence of holiness. Imagine taking it upon ourselves to speak in the throne room of God! In a certain texture of religion, perhaps sponsored mainly by librarians, it may be proper to "let all the earth keep silence," in amazed dread (Hab. 2:20). Israel's characteristic way, however, is not to "let all the earth keep silence" but rather to "make a joyful noise." There is something intrinsically boisterous, and from a certain perspective disordered and disruptive, about Israel's praise, eschewing, as it does, docility, passivity, and too much pious reverence.

Moreover, the audaciousness of this act is not only in its outloudness but in its implicit claim, which is so familiar to us that we fail to notice it. Either in an imperative or in a jussive, Israel says, "Bless the Lord," "Magnify the Lord," "Let us glorify the Lord." Of course, the words can be theologically refined or subdued, or even explained away. If the words are taken on their own terms, however, we see that the one speaking praise is the one who blesses, magnifies, and glorifies; and the object of such active verbs is none other than YHWH. In praise, the traffic runs "upstream," as the speaker acts upon God:

- *to bless* is to bestow the power for life;
- *to magnify* is to make large, great, more significant;
- *to glorify* is to make heavy, prominent, weighty.

Praise bestows something upon YHWH, as though YHWH needed or desired or at least received something God does not yet have.

And we give it! In this daring act, in the very act where we do not expect it, the relation with God is deeply redefined. God receives something from us! It is of course against all intentional evangelical theology that we enact something worthy that runs from us to God, whereby God is pleased, honored, gratified, blessed, made bigger or more powerful. In praise, we impinge upon God, daring to mess with God's own character and constitution. This is indeed an arrogant self-assertion. Unless we explain this bald act more piously, it is better that we don't think about it, but just do it. We do in fact do it when we sing praise; and in our doing it, our relation with God is celebrated and, we dare imagine, improved upon.

4. Praise is *an act of "basic trust."* This formula is that of the psychologist Erik Erikson; it alludes to the most foundational confidence a small baby establishes toward its primary caregiver. Praise as "basic trust" is an unqualified sense of buoyancy and stability in knowing that the "other" is unreservedly reliable. Theories of "object relations" have advanced our understanding of this process beyond Erikson, in my judgment, to suggest that such "basic trust" comes from an experience of the other not as powerful and unapproachable but as completely available.[4] If this insight can be applied to the God/worshiper relation, then I suggest that "basic trust" enacted in worship arises because the singer-speaker of praise has found the one praised to be completely available. That is, the basic trust necessary to full praise arises out of intimate, genuinely covenantal communion in which the one praised has been put at risk, placed under test, and found adequate. The one praised is indeed a reliable other.

5. Praise is thus *a knowing act*. This point follows from the preceding one. An outsider might regard praise as a cold, distant, routine action because in and of itself, praise is voiced as an objective transaction filled with cliches. Indeed, liturgy that is "objective" about God tends to specialize in praise. By terming praise "a knowing act,"

I mean that the moment of praise arises out of a long and troubled history, and it is a hard-won verdict.

In an analysis of the genre of hymns and psalms in general, Claus Westermann has shown that praise is characteristically the conclusion of "plea" (i.e., complaint, lament).[5] What concludes in praise does not begin in praise. It begins rather in hurt, rage, need, indignation, isolation, and abandonment. Israel's first speech to God is not a speech of wonder but of deep need. Israel's primal utterance is not one of celebration or confession but an impatient, insistent protest.[6] It is not submissive adoration but abrasive assertion. It is not an abdication of rights in the presence of God but an affirmation of legitimate need. In that act of insistent assertion, the speaker appropriates, enacts, and constitutes a speaking self. In this act of self-definition, the speaker discovers that he or she can be intimate with God, that God can be addressed, impinged upon, intruded upon, put at risk, placed in jeopardy, and changed. The lament-complaint act dares to assault God and to notice God's lack of attentiveness. It takes courage to pray in this way.[7]

When, however, God is put at risk by such speech and forced to change, then God is found to be, known to be, and forced to be, faithful, as God indeed was not faithful at the beginning of the conversation. That is, "basic trust" is not arrived at by resignation, passivity, or blind acceptance but by testing, demanding insistence. The moment of the turn from "plea" to "praise" (as Westermann has shown) is the moment when God has been brought to new fidelity. Now God can be praised, because God has been pressed to stability, adequacy, responsiveness, and fidelity. Not only is God known to be trustworthy, but the assault of Israel has required God to become more reliable than heretofore, just as a caregiver might not be reliable but is made so by the insistence of the baby. It has taken the risking of self to establish the faithful character of God. It has taken the full assertion of self to bring God to worthy praise.

6. The process of "basic trust" begins in such a painful knowing and audacious assertion. It culminates in praise as *a doxological act*.[8] By "doxological act," I refer to the dialectical alternative of self-assertion, which now becomes glad self-abandonment without reservation, a self-abandonment in which God has become—in this moment of glorification, blessing, and magnification—everything,

and I as the speaker am glad to be nothing. My arrival at doxological self-abandonment, however, comes not out of emptiness but out of fullness, not out of fear but out of buoyant confidence, not out of resignation but out of *chutzpah*.

The doxological act of self-abandonment, done completely without grudge, is the culmination of the process in which there has been testing, risk, and now resolution. This process is not unlike the painful, ongoing quarrel of parent and child that is worked out in anguished candor, or the power struggle between married partners that may culminate in harmony, even if it is momentary and unstable. If that high-risk outcome is finally wrought, those who see the happy outcome know nothing and need know nothing about the struggle on the way. The partners do not need to talk all the time about the hard struggle, do not need to exhibit their shared anguish to the neighbors or to the nations. The history that culminates in self-abandoning basic trust continues always to be present and poignant. Both parties remember it well and have it available.

It is that painful, costly remembering, now done in gratitude and unflinching courage, that lets the doxology be unqualified. Both parties, however, know that the move from pain and plea to praise is not a one-time, irreversible gain. Rather this wondrous act of doxological self-abandonment in trust always keeps at the ready self-assertion voiced in rage. This second option for the relation (an option of rage and alienation) does not diminish or cloud the full doxology. At the same time, however, those who know the tortured career of basic trust are never so naive as not to know that an alternative language is available and at the ready.

Thus basic trust includes both self-abandonment and self-assertion. Praise is a happy settlement that should be taken at full value. It is always, however, a provisional settlement, because even such glad praise does not cause either party to forget what it has taken to arrive at this moment. (I may note in passing that in too much church theology and church liturgy, that painful history of communication is reduced to confession of sin, when in Israel's most knowing texts, the problem is not Israel's sin but God's doubtful and unreliable fidelity. The matter of adjudication between human sin and God's infidelity belongs to the hard work yet to be completed between Christians and Jews, for Christians regularly take all the blame for things not working; conversely, Jews can entertain the notion that the malfunction may indeed be the fault of God.)

The doxological act is an act of gladly ceding all of life in gratitude over to this God.[9] Having fought through the struggles, doxology now freely utters the name, gladly speaks a joyous "you," gladly sounds the adjectives, attributes, and characteristics of this God, and gladly credits this God with all the goodness of life.[10] Thus Israel's doxology is a massive, comprehensive, determined "Hallelujah." "Praise Yah," the one, the real one, the only one from whom all blessings flow.

7. This doxological act of praise is at the same time and inevitably *a polemical act*.[11] That is, the exclusive celebration of this God constitutes a necessary dismissal of every rival claim. There is something passionately monotheizing about doxological speech that credits all to God.[12] Thus the psalm can assert in a series of summonses:

> Sing to YHWH,
> Sing to YHWH,
> Sing to YHWH,
> Tell of YHWH's salvation,
> Declare the glory of YHWH. (Ps. 96:1–3)

There is a determined dismissal of all other gods. When the church says the name of YHWH out loud, under its breath it also says quietly but undoubtedly, "and not Baal, not Marduk, not Dagon, not Enlil, not, not, not." Doxology to YHWH attacks the claim of every other god and every other loyalty. Israel freely confesses that the other gods have no gifts to give, no benefits to bestow, no summons to make, no allegiance to claim. They are massively and forcefully dismissed.

Thus praise is a determined assault on the idols, that is, on loyalties that are declared to be without merit or substance. In Psalm 96, after the fivefold summons to praise YHWH, the next theme is an attack on the idols:

> All the gods of the peoples are idols.
> v. 5

Doxology regularly makes a decisive break with all other loyalties.[13]

To the extent that the idols are assaulted, doxology also implies a critique of every ideology, every claim of truth that moves away from the will and purpose of YHWH. It is relatively easy for us to imagine the dismissal of ancient godly rivals. It is a more difficult contemporary matter to recognize that the alternatives to YHWH in our time and idiom are not nameable gods but "isms" of all kinds that want our loyalty and chase after our life commitment. In our social context, some of the more seductive of these idolatries are consumerism, militarism, ageism, racism, sexism, and capitalism. Praise is a dismissal of every such claim, on both right and left as well as in the complacent center, both sociopolitical and psychopersonal. Doxology critiques and breaks every loyalty that would put a hedge of vested interest between us and the God who invites us to dangerous communion. This means that, when rightly understood, praise itself is a dangerous act of social protest, social criticism, and social delegitimation.

8. It follows then that the doxological, polemical act of praise is inevitably *a political act*, for it concerns authority, power, loyalty, and the right to define reality. The church has a long history of wanting to imagine that praise (or any worship by the church) is a compartmentalized act that does not touch things economic, political, or public. Escapist liturgy imagines that God-talk can be kept from the realities of power. Popularly, that yearning to make praise escapist comes expressed in this way: "Why not keep to religion, and stay out of economics and politics, which are not your proper concern or your expertise?"

That of course is impossible. Formally, Karl Marx has seen that every statement about God inevitably carries with it implicit statements about political power and economic advantage.[14] Long before Marx, however, the prophets of Israel had made the substantive (and not merely formal) point that the character of this God is intimately and unavoidably linked to a passion for well-being, communal justice, human dignity, and health for the creation. One cannot speak of this God, even in doxology, without speaking about that pervasive public agenda. Wherever this God goes, these sovereign concerns are enunciated. Wherever this God is praised, this agenda spills over into the speech of the community and into public life. Wherever this

God is named, social possibility is envisioned. Wherever this God is remembered, political processes are pushed in specific directions. It cannot be otherwise, because of the character of God. Israel's political agenda is no later addendum to praise. This is no "add-on" of social ideology. The God of the Bible is relentlessly a political character whose presence delegitimates wrong power arrangements, whose purposes summon and authorize new power arrangements. Whenever the church gathers for the right praise of the God of the Bible, it willy-nilly engages in such a political insistence that cannot be contained in the safe environs of religion.

9. This act that is doxological, polemical, and political is inherently *a subversive act*. That is, speech that focuses upon the sovereign rule and faithful purpose of this God is odd, unaccommodating speech. It makes no alliance and no epistemological concession but recognizes in its utterance that this rhetoric is an act of guerrilla warfare.[15] That is, this statement of sovereignty moves in the category of miracle, or, as Martin Buber says, it expresses "an abiding astonishment."[16] It celebrates, acknowledges, and claims gifts and purposes that the world judges to be impossible. In its utterance of impossibility, it mocks and dismisses the conventional notions of possibility in which we trust too much. Thus praise, in asserting that new reality emerges around the character of this God, engages in an act of iconoclasm and delegitimation.

We depart from a session of praise less sure of our settled convictions. Corporately, when we sing of YHWH as the lover of justice and peace and freedom, we subvert all power relations that depend upon injustice, hostility, and bondage. Personally, when we sing of dignity and wholeness, we subvert all self-definitions that depend upon crippling self-abasement, destructive self-aggrandizement, and insidious fragmentation. When the song is finished, false modes of self-definition and false construals of neighbor relations are shattered. Such subversiveness brings with it a large share of displacement and disorientation, for it is the destabilization and delegitimizing of what we have most treasured.

It is also like a new breath of life, a new break of day, a new possibility, a resurrection, which lets life be reorganized in utterly obedient, utterly liberated ways. Indeed, the act of praise is the assertion that none of our deathly fixities need have any credence. As practitioners of this praise have always known and confessed, new life begins from doxology and moves out into every sphere of life, for it is nothing other than life that flows from God's own throne room out to the regions where life is still under severe adjudication.[17]

10. Praise as a political, polemical, subversive act in the end is *an evangelical act*. That is, praise is an act whereby the news and claim and possibility of the gospel are enacted.[18] Note well that I say "enacted," not simply summarized from elsewhere. This moment of praise is the moment of redemption. The work and claim of the gospel are not yet finished. Karl Barth, and much more recently Jon Levenson, have shown that the Bible knows that God's new victory has not yet everywhere prevailed.[19] There are still zones and regions of creation that have not yet submitted to the liberating, healing governance of YHWH. Either a glance at the newspaper or an inventory of our own lives makes the point unmistakably clear.[20] Much of our life thus far refuses the rule of this God.

Doxology is an act that submits more and more of life to the rule of this new governance, submitted in glad obedience, submitted in great yearning and in great expectation. "Humanity at praise" (which is one way to define the church), sometimes eagerly, sometimes grudgingly, sometimes fearfully, lets God's governance have its wondrous way. It is an act of "letting go" and, in the glad letting go, finding everything generously shared and richly available. The God who requires radical allegiance is the God who hands everything over to us.

11. In the end—not before, but in the end—praise is *a useless act*.[21] It aims at nothing. It leads to nothing. It intends nothing. It requires nothing. It is not a means but an end in itself, intending nothing other than its own action, which is strangely lacking in substance. As the Westminster Catechism states, our true end is "to glorify and enjoy God." Indeed, it belongs to this relation with this sovereign governor who gives to us far more abundantly than we ask or think, that all our political, polemical acts are superseded. Praise is simply an act of communion that has no purpose other than engagement in this right relation. It is an act of extravagant homecoming when "we come down where we ought to be." That is all, and that is enough.

Notice, in saying this, however, what a deep claim is made. To say that our quintessential human act is not production of anything but is only extravagant communion, is to define our character and purpose in a most eccentric way, a way that breaks with the production-consumption ideology all around us. To focus on this extravagant communion as the purpose of life is to assert an outrageous destiny of repentance and reconciliation in which we enact a radical vision of true self, true communion, true world, true creation; not escapism, but an arrival, for the length of the song, at true destiny.

The church in its praise thus enacts on behalf of the world the true character of the world in the presence of God. It dares to assert and insist that a self fully abandoned to God is in the moment of abandonment a fully confirmed self, and a world fully abandoned to God is a fully confirmed world—a self and a world now marked and authorized for their own proper way in the world where God rules.

Questions for Reflection

1. Have you ever experienced a moment in praise or worship where you could say you fully "ceded your life over to God"? How would you describe it? How was it distinct from other experiences in worship? What words—if any—were part of this experience of doxological praise?

2. How has praise arisen "out of a long and troubled history" as "a hard-won verdict" for you or your community? What have been the moments of painful knowing that—through their remembering—led to your basic trust in God's fidelity?

3. What does a glance at today's newspaper or a courageous inventory of your life, even a brief one, reveal about the work yet to be done to enact the "pervasive public agenda" of the rule of God?

4. Which elements of the act of praise listed below do you see most clearly reflected in your faith community's worship? Which need more attention in order to declare and embody the radical vision of a world fully abandoned to God?

   • liturgical
   • poetic
   • audacious
   • basic trust

- knowing
- doxological
- polemical
- political
- subversive
- evangelical
- useless

Chapter 5

Praise and the Psalms

A Politics of Glad Abandonment, Part Two

On the basis of the previous chapter, I want now to consider some specific cases in which the church, as "humanity at praise," enacts its doxological, polemical, political, subversive, evangelical faith. The Psalter concludes with six hymns of praise that seem designed to bring Israel's faith to a statement of unalloyed "basic trust."[1] This concluding element of the Psalter is liturgical, poetic, audacious, and, in the end, utterly without utilitarian value. I suggest simply that if these so-familiar hymns are taken seriously by the church, a new public world will indeed be enacted.

I

I shall comment on four of these concluding psalms, three briefly and one more extensively.

1. *Psalm 145.*[2] This psalm speaks of God's hidden, powerful providential care that is at work in, with, and under all the circumstances and exigencies of human travail. In a regularized cadence, human need is acknowledged, but in each case it is immediately overridden by God's generosity. The most eloquent statement is rooted in Israel's oldest confession of God's fidelity (Ps. 145:8–9; see Exod. 34:6–7). It is filled with utterly trusting participles that testify to God's enduring, reliable actions. This psalm, a statement of God's powerful providence, is voiced in simplicity, something like an innocent table prayer:

> The eyes of all look to you,
>   and you give them their food in due season.
> You open your hand,
>   satisfying the desire of every living thing.
>   Ps. 145:15–16

In this utterance, Israel at praise (and the church in its wake) dares to assert that all of life is held within God's sustaining governance. What it takes to live is only eyes to look, hands to open, and desires to be satisfied. Notice that the one with looking eyes and open hands and yearning desire does nothing, produces nothing, earns nothing, manipulates nothing, possesses nothing—only gladly, trustingly receives. How dare we in our affluence sing such innocence? Such singing is credible among us only when the singing community turns from its close management, its anxious acquisitiveness, its too careful reckoning, in order to confess that it needs or wants nothing not generously given by God.

The psalm is an evangelical act that invites a deep departure from the greed system of self-securing, nothing less than a redefinition of reality against our crippling ideologies. Humanity at praise says back in confidence to its Lord the dominical assurance that had affirmed:

> Therefore, I tell you, do not worry about your life, what you will eat or what you will drink, or about your body, what you will wear. Is not life more than food, and the body more than clothing? . . . And can any of you by worrying add a single hour to your span of life? And why do you worry about clothing? . . . Therefore do not worry, saying, "What will we eat?" or "What will we drink?" or "What will we wear?" For it is the Gentiles who strive for all these things; and indeed your heavenly Father knows that you need all these things. (Matt. 6:25–32)

In such a universe of discourse, basic trust—like a little sparrow nested with a waiting, open mouth—spills over into issues of food and clothing and housing and access and dignity, inviting a reordered, redistributed human community. It is made possible and made necessary only by the truth of God's giving. Seek one thing; all the rest will follow.

2. *Psalm 149.* This psalm is exceedingly problematic because, after a celebrative introduction (Ps. 149:1–4), it combines "praise the LORD" with "pass the ammunition":

> Let the high praises of God be in their throats
> and two-edged swords in their hands.
>
> Ps. 149:6

After this awkward combination comes a harsh statement about executing vengeance and punishment, about binding kings in fetters and merchant-lords in iron shackles (149:7–9). Anthony Ceresko has proposed, rightly in my judgment, that the psalm moves from a lyrical remembering of *the exodus* to a powerful resolve for *the conquest*, for the seizure of the land of promise.[3] No doubt this theme of land conquest is an embarrassment for us because of its implied rapacious violence. I cite the psalm for two reasons. First, it is a stunning example of how praise engenders public policy, public resolve, and public action. In a less benign form, this psalm is not unlike the great civil rights protests in the United States in the 1960s, which began characteristically in singing and prayer and thus gained courage for public testimony. This psalm shows us Israel at praise, gathering its courage and resolve in order to enact and receive its promise.

Second, the peculiar, critical public action that is here proposed and undertaken is of a very particular kind. It is not violence envisioned against any general population but is precisely against kings and merchant-lords. That is, it is action aimed against those who control a social monopoly and who thereby deny and deprive others of their legitimate goods for life. The worship of the God of the exodus leads to energy and imagination for the righting of social wrong rooted in monopoly and oppression.[4] The psalm is a harsh one; it is nonetheless clear evidence, placed near the liturgical climax of the Psalter, that praise is deeply and directly linked to serious and critical public policy and practice. And if this psalm turns out to be too dangerous to sing in our more bourgeois liturgies, then we may want to consider how such liturgy becomes innocuous and cuts God off from God's deeply rooted social intention.

3. *Psalm 150.* This psalm, the final one, is the extreme case of inutility. It asks nothing. Indeed it almost claims nothing. It nearly says

nothing. It is almost empty form, with a dozen or so summonses to praise, mobilizing all of creation in praise, including the entire temple orchestra. The psalm is the culmination of glad self-abandonment in utter trust, so that all of life comes eagerly under this rule of YHWH. It is worth noting the odd, final juxtaposition of Psalms 149 and 150: a psalm of public resolve and assertion with a psalm of complete abandonment. The pairing of these two psalms is not unlike the juxtaposition of Psalm 1, with its complete devotion to God, and Psalm 2, with its political resolve. Use of the Psalter holds together high liturgical devotion and intense political resolve. Because both belong together in the character of YHWH, both belong inalienably to the praise of Israel. Humanity at praise is at once unreservedly poetic and unapologetically subversive. The music of the church must be endlessly concerned with this definitional juxtaposition.

4. *Psalm 146*. After considering Psalm 145 on hidden providence, Psalm 149 on political resolve, and Psalm 150 on liturgical abandonment in trust, I come to Psalm 146, which brings these three themes together in a wondrous lyric.

Psalm 146 begins with a summons to praise (v. 1), followed by a double resolve by the speaker to praise (v. 2). Praise will last as long as life itself. There will be, for this singer, no "post-praise" existence; praise and life are coterminal. After the introduction of verses 1–2, the psalm becomes moderately didactic. In a sapiential form, the psalm issues a negative warning out of experience. The question of the psalm is: whom shall we trust? The answer is: do not trust princes, do not trust "Adam," do not trust humanity, do not trust creation, do not trust ostensive power. The reason one should not risk such trust is that the "wind" (*ruah*) of the prince and of humanity departs. When the wind leaves the powerful, they die. They become powerless, futile, helpless, unable to deliver, and unable to keep promises. In an affluent society like ours, besotted with self-sufficiency, the question of basic trust is a profound public issue. The negative answer to the question of trust is an assault on the most powerful ideologies of our own society.

The positive counterpart to the warning in verses 3–4 begins with a sapiential formula, "Happy are those . . ." (v. 5). They are lucky, fortunate. The rulers of this age are of no help; the God of Jacob, by contrast, is a real help, utterly reliable, and capable of making a difference. Then the sapiential form moves abruptly into a large, sweeping doxology, dominated (as in Ps. 145) with participles that testify to God's characteristic, most reliable actions. This creator God, the one who originates and bestows the very wind of life upon which powerful people necessarily rely, this God is the one who keeps *hesed* forevèr, who is utterly reliable. This God, so helpful, is unlike power arrangements of this age, which are fickle and fleeting and unable to help.

There follows in the psalm a bill of particulars concerning the fidelity of this creator God "who makes, who keeps, who executes, who gives." The large claim of creation and of abiding *hesed* moves immediately to justice for the oppressed and food for the hungry. Israel cannot praise YHWH very long without embracing the core agenda of well-being for God's beloved creatures. In this psalm YHWH gives that which Jesus in Matthew 6 removes from our zone of anxiety: food, clothing, and wherewithal for life. This theme keeps emerging in the midst of Israel's most passionate praise of YHWH.

Then the psalm names the Name five times (Ps. 146:7b–9). In naming the Name, the psalm under its breath debunks and dismisses every other name:

- The LORD [not Baal] sets the prisoners free;
- the LORD [not some ruler] opens the eyes of the blind.
- The LORD [not the free-market system or a Western government] lifts up those who are bowed down;
- the LORD [not the church organization] loves the righteous.
- The LORD [not my favorite political persuasion] watches over the strangers, upholds the orphan and the widow.

The doxology draws God and the singing congregation into the reality of social emergency, social inequality, and social possibility. Then comes the concluding doxology that matches the introduction and is played like a high trump card that requires a positive outcome (v. 10).

In this song, humanity at praise has brought YHWH into full character. In singing, at the same time that YHWH is brought into full character, the world has been recharacterized, and the socially invisible ones have been noticed, named, and cared for. The singers are now drawn into a triangle with the God who cares powerfully and with the neighbors who need desperately. The song is an act of strenuous, dangerous imagination. The singing community is left in a new place, there to hone its ethics and to work out its salvation. Praise, like salvation, is done with fear and trembling.

Psalm 146 is a statement about God's powerful purpose for human well-being and so echoes Psalm 145. Psalm 146 is an act of self-abandonment in trust to God as much as is Psalm 150. The psalm urges casting one's lot with this God, who is originary, present, powerful, and noticing, the only true help and comfort in life. Psalm 146 lives at the threshold of action, not as explicitly as does Psalm 149, but tacitly inviting Israel to catch up with the public reality over which God presides. Such singing as Psalm 146 precludes any more dropping out into safe, indulgent self-concern, because the world is decisively reshaped in the song. The sinners cannot stand outside the orbit of YHWH and YHWH's noticed, treasured partners.

Thus the church, at the end of its Psalter, sings these hymns of providence (Ps. 145), policy (Ps. 149), abandonment (Ps. 150), and true help (Ps. 146). In the singing, it finds its world healingly, demandingly reorganized.

Now, finally, a practical comment. My urging is an embarrassingly simple and obvious one. Behind human management lies liberated imagination.[5] Behind memo lies poetry. Behind money stands mouth. In its praise, the church is big-mouthed. This company of singers must find its mouth and its voice, and then put its money where its mouth is. It will not, however, put its money in daringly new places in passionate new ways until its mouth, its tongue, is put unreservedly at the disposal of this God.

On mouth and money, consider two conversations in the story of Jesus. In Mark 10:17–22, there is an exchange with a rich man. The rich man puts a question to Jesus: "What must I do with my money?" Or more familiarly, "Good Teacher, what must I do to inherit eternal life?" His is a reasoned voice, wanting a reasoned answer, wanting to make studied, calculated decisions about the future. You know the outcome of the conversation. After an exchange about commandments he has already obeyed, the man goes away still in possession of his possessions. And then follows some evangelical talk about possessions and camels and needles.

At the end of the same Mark 10, there is the blind beggar Bartimaeus (vv. 46–52). The beggar pushes his way into the presence of Jesus, even against the crowd that tries to silence him. Twice Bartimaeus uses his voice and cries out demandingly. The beggar will not be silenced. He cries out, he insists, he demands, much to the embarrassment of the onlookers. He forces Jesus to do a healing. When he is healed, he signs on for the mission of Jesus.

The contrast between the two men in the same chapter of Mark is almost too easy. Nonetheless, notice the interface between *mouth* and *money*. The first man with much money wanted to tone down the speech of the gospel to keep it controlled and without danger. The second man is a beggar, that is, without money, but with a loud, shrill, liberated mouth. And he comes to healing. I suppose for well-kept people who inhabit much of the Western church, the question is whether our money will tone down our mouth, or if, in the face of presumed self-sufficiency, our mouth, in protest and demand, in gratitude and amazement, can break toward newness with our money. God first wants not money but mouths—speech, utterance, testimony—to evoke new reality. And from such speech comes action in the world.

II

1. In his poem "Providence," George Herbert speaks of the human vocation of praise:

> Of all the creatures both in sea and land
> Only to Man thou hast made known thy ways,
> And put the pen alone into his hand,
> And made him *secretary of thy praise*.

> Beasts fain would sing; birds ditty to their notes;
> Trees would be tuning on their native lute
> To thy renown: but all their hands and throats
> Are brought to man, while they are lame and mute.

> Man is the *world's high priest*: he doth present
> The sacrifice for all; while they below
> Unto the service mutter an assent,
> Such as springs use that fall, and winds that blow.

He that to praise and laud thee doth refrain,
Doth not refrain unto himself alone,
But robs a thousand who would praise thee fain,
And doth commit a world of sin in one.

The beasts say, Eat me: but, if beasts must teach,
The tongue is yours to eat, but mine to praise.
The trees say, Pull me: but the hand you stretch,
Is mine to write, as it is yours to raise.

Wherefore, most sacred Spirit, I here present
For me and all my fellows praise to thee:
And just it is that I should pay the rent,
Because the benefit accrues to me.[6]

I simply remind you:

you—secretary of praise;
you—world's high priest;
you—upon whom all the creatures depend, upon whose tongue
    all creatures great and small depend for proper doxology;
you—to keep the mystery functioning;
you—to keep God blessed, glorified, magnified;
you—to let this holy Thou be Thou among us.

Everything depends upon your courage to engage finally in this subversive, useless act that lets the world be the world God intends. It is time for "the secretary" to read the minutes.

2. Daniel W. Hardy and David F. Ford conclude their fine book on praise urging joyous praise against a joyless stoicism. They refer to the "jazz factor" in authentic praise.[7] They know that in jazz, "order gives play to non-order," that "the jazz factor can inspire a newly improvised future." They recall that jazz is irrepressible, that it arose in "slave Christianity," which dared to push beyond known, settled reality for the sake of God's new impossibilities. Think of churches as humanity at praise, in praise letting order give play to nonorder, in liturgy letting a newly improvised future rise!

You see, we are in an emergency that our technological self-sufficiency and our tight management cannot solve, but can only deepen. The church, humanity at praise, may create an infrastructure of evangelical imagination out of which can arise new socioeconomic, human possibility.

In his book on jazz, Gene Lees describes the moment of making jazz as follows:

> Making jazz is a very naked thing to do. That anyone can do anything at all but stand there in paralyzed amazement when the chord changes are going by, that musicians can function with minimal premeditation and great creativity within the materials of a song's structure, is more remarkable than even the most expert practitioners themselves seem to appreciate. It requires both tremendous knowledge, whether intuitive or acquired, and the physical reflexes of an athlete. Jazz is not only one of the most remarkable achievements in the history of music, it is one of the most striking achievements in the history of human thought.[8]

What a moment in the church and in creation, when the church sings its way into an improvised fresh future! Such praise is one of the most striking achievements in the history of human utterance. When we sing, we are humanity at praise, when all the trumpets and lutes and strings and pipes of Psalm 150 break out in this "naked act." What a moment when George Herbert's beasts—storks and birds and wild goats and coneys and young lions and wild asses—all break out in new improvisation.[9] What a moment when all the noticed ones of Psalm 146—prisoners, the blind, the bowed down, strangers, widows, and orphans—find their daring voice. What a moment when creation gets its voice for its proper, dangerous work. It is a moment of threat and of healing, of breaking down and building up, of weeping and laughing, mourning, dancing, throwing away and keeping, of seeking and losing.[10] It is a joyful noise—for all things new.

3. We are at a break point in Western culture, besotted as we are with economic self-sufficiency, political triumphalism, and ideological arrogance. In the midst of that self-sufficiency, triumphalism, and arrogance, we are in a deep emergency. The emergency is the shriveling of the human spirit, the decline of the human infrastructure, and the disappearance of human imagination. That shriveling, decline, and disappearance correlate with technological ascendancy and are manifested in fatigue, anxiety, despair, amnesia, numbness, and finally in brutality.

I do not imagine that the larger emergency can be resolved by the liturgists and musicians of the church. I do nonetheless conclude that those who "script" the imagination of the church have crucial and distinctive roles to play in this emergency. In its numbed desperation, our culture now waits for voices that can utter the subversive news, that can practice honest criticism and sound serious hurt, that can evoke human courage and energy out beyond our fearful vested interest.

The work to be done is not "mere" church worship; it is rather the lyrical, relentless claim of our praising humanness. In a jazz act of sub-version, of self-abandonment toward trustfulness, this humanity at praise could practice God's dangerous promise and presence. Everything depends on a joyful noise, sounded through our bodies and past our fears, to newness.

Questions for Reflection

1. Psalm 145 gives voice to a grateful community in the trustworthy hands of a God who provides, which results in a more just and equitable distribution of resources for all. How would the world be different if we took seriously the promise and vision of this psalm's words?

2. Psalm 149 moves from "praise the LORD" to "pass the ammunition." How does this movement—from praise to public policy and action against oppressive systems and rulers—relate to this moment in history? What does our discomfort with its recitation in our liturgy say about us and our usual uses of praise?

3. Psalm 150 exemplifies the form of praise that accomplishes nothing save calling all creation to also praise. How does the pairing of this devotional psalm with the subversive one preceding it challenge our use of the Psalter in our liturgy?

4. Psalm 146 brings into a triangle of relationship the singer, God who cares powerfully about a reordered world, and neighbors in desperate need. Brueggemann calls this an act of "dangerous imagination" set in a time of great emergency. Where do you see the church beginning to improvise a new future in "jazz acts of sub-version"?

Chapter 6

Doxology

The Creator Toys with Monster Chaos (Psalm 104)

1. An Inventory Framed by Doxology

Psalm 104 is likely the longest and most lyrical biblical text on creation. It divides roughly into two parts. The first (vv. 1–24) provides an inventory of the components of creation, framed by a doxological formula. *Inventory framed by doxology* is a good way to begin thinking about creation.

The inventory of verses 2–23 moves from the largest elements of creation to the most concrete and particular. It begins with the three-storied world that is conventional in ancient texts: the heavens (vv. 2–4), the earth (vv. 5–9), and the waters beneath the earth (vv. 10–13). Each receives due doxological attention signaled by the "you" of the creator as generous agent:

> *You* stretch out the heavens. (v. 2)
> *You* set the earth on its foundations. (v. 5)
> *You* make springs gush forth in the valleys. (v. 10)

Without detracting from the wonders of the creatures, the doxology easily moves past the creatures to the creator, who is the real subject of the whole.

After the "big three" of heavens/earth/waters, the inventory becomes more specific. The outcome of this well-ordered system of generativity consists of

> Grass for the cattle,
> Food from the earth,

Wine to gladden the heart,
Oil to make the face shine, and
Bread to strengthen the heart. (vv. 14–15)

These elemental gifts constitute the necessities of life, the prerequisites for a viable, sustainable, joyous human community: food, wine, oil, and bread!

In verses 16–23, the doxology provides a ready list of creatureliness:

Trees,
Birds,
Wild goats and coneys,
Moon and sun,
Night for the animals who seek prey,
Day for the animals to withdraw into safe rest, and
People (*'adam*) who do work.

The sweep from trees, birds, and animals to humankind, all in an ordered rhythm of day and night, is terse and buoyant, paralleling the movement of creative acts in Genesis 1. The inventory of the big three (Ps. 104:2–13), the elemental requirements for sustenance (vv. 14–15), and a map of "all creatures" (vv. 16–23) constitutes, in sum, a working, sustainable system of life.

This inventory is framed in doxology. The divine name is uttered in verse 1 and again in verse 24, at the conclusion. In between is the incidental reference to "trees of the LORD" in verse 16, which is not rhetorically significant. Thus, verses 1–24 reveals a symmetry of doxological framing:

Bless *the LORD*, O my soul.
O LORD my God, you are very great.
You are clothed with honor and majesty,
    wrapped in light as with a garment. . . .
O LORD, how manifold are your works!
    In wisdom you have made them all;
    the earth is full of your creatures.
            vv. 1–2a, 24, emphasis added

The concluding doxology in verse 24 bursts with awed enthusiasm concerning "your works, you have made them, your creatures." It is all "you, you, you," to whom the creation is referred. The repeated use of *you* gladly affirms that the world is not autonomous in either self-sufficiency or deficit, and gladly refers back to YHWH, on whom the singing community is focused. Both the *withholding* and the *utterance* of the divine name thus reflect artistic intentionality and communicate theologically.

2. Creation and Chaos

In the second half of the poem (verses 25–35), we can trace four themes that refer to the paradigmatic power and significance of creation. The first theme is *creation and chaos*, which is sounded in praise:

> Yonder is the sea, great and wide,
>   creeping things innumerable are there,
>   living things both small and great.
> There go the ships,
>   and Leviathan that you formed to sport in it.
>   vv. 25–26

At the center of these verses are "innumerable creeping things . . . great and small"! Israel notices and values every one, affirming the care and precision of the creator. The creatures "beyond count" may be measured by the stars of the heavens or the sand of the seashore or the heirs promised to Abraham and Sarah. The whole of the earth and its inhabitants attest to the life-giving capacity of YHWH.

That notion of "great and small" is bounded in these verses by bigger forces. At the outset is "the sea, great and wide." Israel acknowledges the sea, but knows that it is best kept at a distance. The sea is beyond the edge of safety, beyond the land of promise. While Israel knows it as threat, in doxology Israel can say that this unnamed force is also a creature of YHWH. Thus, in the exodus tradition, YHWH uses the mighty waters as a vehicle to override the forces of bondage for emancipation. In the Song of Moses, YHWH uses the sea to subdue Pharaoh:

> Pharaoh's chariots and his army he cast into the sea;
>   his picked officers were sunk in the Red Sea.
> The floods covered them;

> they went down into the depths like a stone. . . .
> At the blast of your nostrils the waters piled up,
>   the floods stood in a heap;
>   the deeps congealed in the heart of the sea.
>
> Exod. 15:4–5, 8

Before such a force, Pharaoh is helpless:

> You blew with your wind, the sea covered them;
>   they sank like lead in the mighty waters.
>
> v. 10

Israel can boast about the ferocious power of the sea that yields in fear before the creator. And even the Jordan River can be a surrogate for that fearful chaotic-turned-obedient sea:

> The sea looked and fled;
>   Jordan turned back. . . .
> Why is it, O sea, that you flee?
> O Jordan, that you turn back?
>
> Ps. 114:3, 5

And Israel uses the same language to speak of homecoming from Babylon:

> Thus says the LORD,
>   who makes a way in the sea,
>   a path in the mighty waters,
> who brings out chariot and horse,
>   army and warrior;
> they lie down, they cannot rise,
>   they are extinguished, quenched like a wick:
> Do not remember the former things,
>   or consider the things of old.
>
> Isa. 43:16–17

Jonah, too, narrates his forced plunge into the sea, after YHWH threw his recalcitrant servant into that terrifying threat; but of course Jonah is "brought up" by YHWH (Jonah 2:3–6). Even in the temple, Israel sings of the way that the sea, along with other creatures, welcomes the rule of YHWH:

Let the heavens be glad, and let the earth rejoice;
  let the sea roar, and all that fills it;
  let the field exalt, and everything in it.

Ps. 96:11

The sea at the beginning is matched at the end by Leviathan, the great sea monster, already said to have been created by YHWH in Genesis 1:21. Leviathan is part of what makes the sea such a surging threat. Israel remembers, however, how God domesticated Leviathan:

You divided the sea by your might;
  you broke the heads of the dragons in the waters.
You crushed the heads of Leviathan;
  you gave him as food for the creatures of the wilderness.

Ps. 74:13–14

In Job 41, YHWH even brags about Leviathan, "king over all that are proud" (Job 41:34). The creator naturally knows all the details of its design, its double coat of mail (v.13), its teeth (v. 14), its eyelids (v. 18), its nostrils (v. 20), its neck and heart—all told, so ferocious that

It makes the deep boil like a pot;
  it makes the sea like a pot of ointment.

v. 31

Human agents, warns the creator, cannot handle it:

Lay hands on it;
  think of the battle; you will not do it again!

v. 8

The poetry permits us to feel the threat, terror, and awesomeness of the mightiest force in the surging waters. But in Psalm 104, Leviathan is but a toy for YHWH, "formed [for] sport" (v. 26), designed to make YHWH laugh in delight.

The substantive issue in all this is chaos. The threat is a surging wildness not yet brought under control. Four points are crucial here:

1. The threat of chaos has been present in Israel's sensibility since before day one, because it is found already in Genesis 1:2 as *tohu*

wabohu, "formless and void." Creation is not ex nihilo, but an act of imposed order, form, shape, and purpose on the seething reality of "precreation." That form is wrought not by power and conflict but by due authority, the kind of authority a doctor works on an anxious patient, or a pastor works on bereaved family, or a youth pastor works on a middle-school student, or a poet works amid revolutionary fervor. Such analogues work only to give us a taste of the disorder that characterizes creaturely life, and the order, limit, boundary, and separation, all the acts that bring sanity and worldly possibility from the will of God.

2. The reference to Leviathan bespeaks an active force of chaos, not only disorder but an agent that intends to cause disorder in God's creation. In his treatment of *das Nichtige*, Karl Barth insists on the ontic reality of nothingness as the evil and death that attack creatures directly, the creator indirectly. That power that seeks to negate is other than both creature and creator.[1] After many pages describing the reality and threat of nothingness, Barth unsurprisingly concludes that even nothingness is one of the things that works together for the good of those that love God (Rom. 8:28). Consequently, Barth can say that nothingness can be viewed, in retrospect, only as a force that threatened but has been overcome. In this, Barth echoes Psalm 104:26.

3. We must be honest, however, and admit that the negating force of chaos continues to be with us. We know in elemental ways that our life is under threat. After we have taken the measure of Communists or terrorists or immigrants or Muslims (or whatever else is a convenient enmity for us), we are bound to say that in the middle of the night, it is raw, unadorned chaos—the surging sea, the incomprehensible dragon, the devouring monster—that haunts, wakes, or terrifies us.

But consider Israel! In buoyant doxology, Israel acknowledges the monster but promptly and firmly demotes it from world-devouring threat to just(!) a majestic creature who in fact is no threat at all—just one of God's many works, ultimately God's plaything. The world will hold, then, because of the creator who has the whole world in hand.

4. This recurring drama of threat and assurance also appears in Mark 4:35–41, where the early church remembered Jesus performing the authoritative work of the creator. The disciples were in a boat, at sea, and at risk in the waters: "A great windstorm arose, and the waves beat into the boat, so that the boat was already being swamped"

(v. 37). This echoes the dilemma of Pharaoh in Exodus 15, Jonah in the belly of the monster, and a common cadence of the Psalter:

> Some went down to the sea in ships,
>   doing business on the mighty waters;
> they saw the deeds of the LORD,
>   his wondrous works in the deep.
> For he commanded and raised the stormy wind,
>   which lifted up the waves of the sea.
> They mounted up to heaven, they went down to the depths;
>   their courage melted away in their calamity;
> they reeled and staggered like drunkards,
>   and were at their wits' end.
>
>   Ps. 107:23–27

We are told that the disciples scolded Jesus for being inattentive to their fear: "Teacher, do you not care that we are perishing?" (Mark 4:38). Jesus responded: "He woke up and rebuked the wind, and said to the sea, 'Peace! Be still!'" (v. 39). This narrative thus explicates Psalm 107:

> They cried to the LORD in their trouble,
>   and he brought them out from their distress;
> he made the storm be still,
>   and the waves of the sea were hushed.
>
>   vv. 28–29

Then Jesus questioned them with rebuke: "Why are you afraid? Have you still no faith?" (Mark 4:40). All they could do was wonder: "Who then is this, that even the wind and sea obey him?" (v. 41).

That is how it is between creator and creature, between trouble and entreaty, between rescue and bewilderment. The taming, ordering work of the creator leaves us in awe that cannot be fully deciphered. Which is why only doxology will do!

3. Creation and Provision

The second theme is *creation and provision*. In Psalm 104, Israel's doxology makes this affirmation to YHWH:

These all look to you
  to give them their food in due season;
when you give it to them, they gather it up;
  when you open your hand, they are filled with good things.
                                                    vv. 27–28

These verses characterize with precision the transaction between creator and creatures, all of them!

All creatures look in expectation for food from you;
all creatures gather it up;
all creatures are filled with good things.

The image is of a satiated, satisfied creation. Of course, it all depends on the "You":

You give them food on a proper schedule;
You give (the verb is repeated);
You open your hand.

The creator "gives, gives, opens"; the creatures "gather, receive, eat," and "are filled." This transaction is endless, reliable, and necessary. The creatures are always on the receiving end of the generous giving of the creator.

And so it is that we constantly celebrate the conviction that creation is the initiation and sustaining of a reliable, abundant food chain for all creatures. It is already asserted in the creation story:

And the LORD God planted a garden in Eden, in the east; and there he put the man whom he had formed. Out of the ground the LORD God made to grow every tree that is pleasant to the sight and good for food, the tree of life also in the midst of the garden, and the tree of the knowledge of good and evil. (Gen. 2:8–9)

Before the narrative accentuates human responsibility for the garden, "to till it and keep it" (v. 15), the text discusses the primal gift of food freely given, without neglecting aesthetic sensibilities. Likewise, the outcome of the first creation story is a teeming, rich, abundant provision of food in which all plants, animals, fish, and birds are provided for, and in which they are themselves engaged in the work of food production (see Gen. 1:20–30). The world is designed for well-being, so that a banquet becomes a metaphor for the goodness of God and the joy of creation.

When we scan the concordance for "food," sooner or later the affirmation of creation as provision of abundant food will lead us to the manna story in Exodus 16. That story is set in the wilderness of scarcity that produced anxiety, complaint, and murmuring. Israel feared for their lives, for *wilderness* in the Bible means a place without viable life-support systems. In their anxiety, the Israelites contrasted their vulnerable circumstances with what they misremembered about Pharaoh's Egypt:

> If only we had meat to eat! We remember the fish we used to eat in Egypt for nothing, the cucumbers, the melons, the leeks, the onions, and the garlic; but now our strength is dried up, and there is nothing at all but this manna to look at. (Num. 11:4–6)

Of course, it was not like that. In Egypt they had only "the bread of affliction" (Deut. 16:3) produced by a pharaoh who was the invariable agent of *anti*-creation. Pharaoh's Egypt was a zone of abusive scarcity where no one could ever be satisfied, joyous, or at rest. In the exodus, then, Israel traded that zone of death for the possibility of wilderness.

After complaint and divine response, Israel discovers that the wilderness too could be transformed by the creator God into a viable creation. They did not understand the inexplicable bread of abundance that was given to them. There was, nevertheless, enough for all: some gathered a little, some gathered more, all had enough (Exod. 16:18). Except some wanted to replicate Pharaoh, even in the wilderness, and so they gathered too much and tried to hoard and monopolize, until they spoiled the whole thing (vv. 20–21). They treated the *abundance of the creation* as though it was the *scarcity of Pharaoh*. The end of the narrative confirms that even this wilderness was within YHWH's zone of reliable creation by mandating Sabbath—restfulness in a circumstance that might otherwise have evoked acute anxiety (vv. 29–30).

No wonder then that Israel's doxology can sing of the ways that the creator God moves into wilderness, the way the food giver moves against *tohu wabohu* and compels, commands, and permits food to surface. So, Israel sings:

> The wilderness and the dry land shall be glad,
>   the desert shall rejoice and blossom;
> like the crocus it shall blossom abundantly,
>   and rejoice with joy and singing.
>
> Isa. 35:1

> I am about to do a new thing;
>   now it springs forth, do you not perceive it?
> I will make a way in the wilderness
>   and rivers in the desert.
> The wild animals will honor me,
>   the jackals and the ostriches;
> for I give water in the wilderness,
>   rivers in the desert,
> to give drink to my chosen people,
>   the people whom I formed for myself
> so that they might declare my praise.
>
> Isa. 43:19–21

The wonder of abundance, always counterintuitive in a world of striving, becomes an antidote to scarcity (see Amos 9:13–14). Indeed, Jesus imagines a fool living like Pharaoh, building more storehouses, tearing down barns in order to build bigger barns (Luke 12:16–21). But then Jesus jerks his disciples back to the truth of creation:

> Therefore I tell you, do not worry about your life, what you will eat, or about your body, what you will wear. For life is more than food, and the body more than clothing. Consider the ravens; they neither sow nor reap, they have neither storehouse nor barn, and yet God feeds them. . . . For it is the nations of the world that strive after all these things, and your Father knows that you need them. (Luke 12:22–24, 30)

Creation becomes an antidote to anxiety, which is the status quo under pharaonic scarcity.

The truth of creation is that we are on the receiving end. Our part in creation then is gratitude, most regularly and reliably done in table prayers, a pause to acknowledge that the meal is a gift from a giver who keeps giving to the just and the unjust. Thus Psalm 104:27–28, quoted above, serves as an apt prayer, and is paralleled in Psalm 145:

> The eyes of all look to you,
>   and you give them their food in due season.
> You open your hand,
>   satisfying the desire of every living thing.
>   vv. 15–16

Prayer before meals is a glad acknowledgment that it is all gift.

The wonder of food freely given and gratefully received stands at the center of Jesus' ministry. Twice Mark reports that Jesus performed the work of the creator in giving abundant food. In Mark 6, Jesus finds his way to "a deserted place" (Mark 6:31), which is to say, a wilderness. Moved to compassion by the hungry crowd (v. 34), he takes what is available—not much—and does his lordly thing with it. He takes the bread, blesses it, breaks the loaves, and gives it to the people. He takes, blesses, breaks, and gives (v. 41). He multiplies the loaves the way creation is commanded to multiply. He feeds five thousand people with twelve baskets remaining, a surplus symbolically enough for all twelve tribes. Jesus does it again in Mark 8. Before a great crowd without anything to eat, moved by compassion, he takes the loaves, gives thanks (*eucharistēsas*), breaks the bread, and gives it (8:1–6). He takes, thanks, breaks, and gives. He feeds four thousand with a perfect, symbolically complete seven baskets remaining. In the following episode, he instructs his disciples about the bread; but they do not see that in this meal the power of the creator has transformed the scarcity and chaos of the wilderness into a livable venue (vv. 14–20). They have no sense that in Jesus the full force of the creator God is at work. Thus Mark sourly and tersely concludes: "They did not understand about the loaves, but their hearts were hardened" (6:52; cf. 8:21).

They missed the disclosure given in the bread because, Mark says, they had hard hearts. They thought like the quintessentially hard-hearted Pharaoh by filtering the wonder of ample bread through the prism of scarcity. Scarcity, rooted in anxiety, is the great alternative to creation. Anxious scarcity evokes no gratitude, but only exploitation and violence. The doxological conviction of Israel is that anxious antineighborly action generates scarcity. Conversely, generous neighborly action evokes the abundant fruitfulness of creation.

No wonder, then, that the church has a meal as the quintessential performance of (re)creation. The bread and wine at Eucharist (that is, at *gratitude*, which is what the Greek term means) constitute the simplest, most elemental act that the church performs. It is, every time, a defiant act of abundance that subverts the world's will to scarcity. We come to the table of generous creation hungry, and we depart filled with bread, gratitude, wine, energy, and courage. At the moment when the pastor hands over bread and wine and says the ancient formulae, creation tingles again with abundance. It is for that reason, I suspect, that in the inventory of Psalm 104, Israel's doxology declares:

> You . . . bring forth *food* from the earth,
>   and *wine* to gladden the human heart,
>   *oil* to make the face shine,
>   and *bread* to strengthen the human heart.
>   vv. 14–15

That's it! *Food, wine, oil, bread!* These are both the quotidian realities of human life, and they are also the deepest sacramental signs, assuring us that we are heirs of the coming banquet and participants in it even now.

4. Creation and *Ruah*

A third theme, *creation and ruah*, is voiced in Psalm 104:29–30:

> When you hide your face, they are dismayed;
>   when you take away their breath, they die
>   and return to their dust.
> When you send forth your spirit, they are created;
>   and you renew the face of the ground.

These verses use the Hebrew word *ruah* twice, once negatively and once positively. The double use is not readily recognized in most translations because in verse 29 it is "breath," whereas it is "spirit" in verse 30. But the same term is used deliberately to state a contrast;

both verses refer to YHWH's generous, life-initiating, life-sustaining gift of vitality, without which no creature can live:

> If he should take back his spirit to himself,
>   and gather to himself his breath,
> all flesh would perish together,
>   and all mortals return to dust.
>
> Job 34:14–15

The ancients were empirical and pragmatic about breath and life. They could see that if one breathed, there was life, and that when one no longer breathed, there was death. They could observe that from birth on, one must inhale before one can exhale, one must receive before one can emit. They could, as children still do, test their breath, seeing how long one could "hold it," but one cannot do so very long. They concluded that breath is a (pre)condition of life, comes to us as a gift, and cannot be owned, possessed, or controlled by us. One is dependent and vulnerable and grateful for the gift that one cannot conjure for one's self. They were able to extend that insight from human persons to all creatures, and thus they readily imagined that plants, fish, and birds also depended on the gift of breath that is God's to give and to withdraw.

The latter, negative possibility is captured in three short lines of poetry in Psalm 104:29:

- God sometimes is hidden and not available, and we are alarmed because the source of life, identity, and safety is not near.
- The second line advances the trouble. The divine withdrawal of *ruah* leads to death.
- The third line closes with our return to dust, as we say on Ash Wednesday. We remember that we are breathed-on dust, animated briefly by *ruah*, but again, at the end, just dust.

The negative poetry is all about dependence. No *ruah*, no life.

The positive counterpoint in verse 30 offers only two lines.

- When you emit *ruah*, they (all creatures) are created (*bara'*). The verb is the same as in Genesis 1:1. It is an act of bringing form and vitality to the formlessness of scattered dust, so that "create" here is the counterpoint to "die in dismay" (Ps. 104:29).

- The second line in verse 30 uses "renew, make utterly new," in parallel with "create." The object of the verb is "the face of the earth," a counterpoint to "dust."

Thus the two verses together refer to:

- *ruah* withdrawn / *ruah* given;
- die in dismay / created;
- dust / ground.

Again, everything depends on YHWH, who is the great, reliable, steadfast iron lung without which the world would revert to *tohu wabohu*.

These verses articulate Israel's creation faith that God's self-giving breath permits the world to have vitality and possibility. Because these verses follow the table prayer of verses 27–28, which refers to all creation, they do not apply solely to humanity. Instead it is a nondescript "they": they are dismayed, they die, they return to the dust, they are created. Humankind has no special claim on these verbs but stands alongside other creatures in dependence and in grateful, amazed doxology.

The same imagery is present in the creation narratives. In Genesis 2, it is not *ruah* but a synonym with the same physiological, theological force:

> Then the LORD God formed man from the dust of the ground, and breathed into his nostrils the *breath of life* [*nishmat hayyim*]; and the man became a living being. (v. 7)

The human person is breathed-on dust, formed by the creator out of formless soil. In Genesis 1, it is God's *ruah* that makes possible living space for the creatures:

> The earth was formless void and darkness covered the face of the deep, while a wind [*ruah*] from God swept over the face of the waters. (v. 2)

The breath of God performs very differently in the two narratives, because Genesis 2 is focused on human destiny, whereas Genesis 1 has a cosmic vista. But the ultimate point is the same as Psalm 104.

All creatures, all created reality, wait to inhale in order to have life. Here there is no self-starting for the creatures, no self-sufficiency or independent possibility. The good news is that none of that self-obsession is necessary because,

> As a father has compassion for his children,
>   so the LORD has compassion for those who fear him.
> For he knows how we were made;
>   he remembers that we are dust.
>
> Ps. 103:13–14

God remembers Genesis 2:7 and knows how we have been formed and how we are created and sustained only by the faithful gifts of the creator.

In light of all that, it is not difficult but quite important to trace the force of *ruah* in creation, which I will do by mentioning six familiar texts, though others could be added.

1. In Isaiah 11:2, the term *ruah* occurs four times:

> The *spirit* of the LORD shall rest on him,
>   the *spirit* of wisdom and understanding,
>   the *spirit* of counsel and might,
>   the *spirit* of knowledge and the fear of the LORD.

The anticipated carrier of the Davidic line envisioned here will at long last be a reliable ruler and judge who will practice justice for the poor and needy. That king for whom Israel waits will act in this way precisely because of the *ruah* of YHWH. The *ruah* blows the king beyond himself to be a generative force for a new world. The *ruah* from YHWH is marked by wisdom, understanding, counsel, might, knowledge, and fear of YHWH. This is no ordinary king, but one who knows better about the deployment of power. This king is festally dressed in "righteousness and faithfulness." This king, furthermore, is not autonomous, as everything depends on YHWH's *ruah*. Verses 6–9 then offer a vision of the new creation in which the earth is full of the knowledge of the Lord. All of that depends on the life-giving force of *ruah*.

2. Psalm 146 celebrates the good rule of YHWH, who does justice for those who are oppressed, prisoners, those who are blind,

strangers, orphans, and widows. All of that generative engagement is contrasted to princes and mortals who are no help:

> Do not put your trust in princes,
>   in mortals, in whom there is no help.
> When their *breath* departs, they return to the earth;
>   on that very day their plans perish.
>
> vv. 3–4

In contrast to Isaiah 11, Psalm 146 makes clear that without God's *ruah*, princes have no staying power and simply return to the soil from which they came. The contrast is between the generative power of God's *ruah* and the absence of all generativity without that *ruah*.

3. In Isaiah 42, YHWH is celebrated as the creator:

> Thus says God, the LORD,
>   who created the heavens and stretched them out,
>   who spread out the earth and what comes from it,
> who gives *breath* [*neshamah*] to the people upon it
>   and *spirit* [*ruah*] to those who walk in it:
> I am the LORD, I have called you in righteousness,
>   I have taken you by the hand and kept you;
> I have given you as a covenant to the people,
>   a light to the nations,
>   to open the eyes that are blind,
> to bring out the prisoners from the dungeons,
>   from the prison those who sit in darkness.
>
> vv. 5–7

Once again, the decisive verb is "create," and the outcome of the gift of *ruah* and *neshamah* is a covenant and a light, and good news for those who are blind and imprisoned. Here, the *ruah* of the creator makes new, neighborly life possible on earth.

4. In Isaiah 61, read by Jesus in Nazareth, the servant's great ministry of emancipation and reconciliation is initiated by the *ruah* of YHWH:

> The *spirit* of the Lord GOD is upon me,
>   because the LORD has anointed me;
> he has sent me to bring good news to the oppressed,
>   to bind up the brokenhearted,

to proclaim liberty to the captives,
    and release to the prisoners;
to proclaim the year of the LORD's favor,
    and the day of vengeance of our God.

vv. 1–2a

The *ruah* designates, empowers, and deploys; and society is made new (v. 3).

5. Ezekiel 37 provides a defining link between creation and resurrection, two tropes for God-given, new life:

I looked, and there were sinews on them, and flesh had come upon them, and skin had covered them; but there was no *breath* [*ruah*] in them. Then he said to me, "Prophesy to the *breath* [*ruah*], prophesy, mortal, and say to the *breath* [*ruah*]: Thus says the Lord GOD: Come from the four winds, O *breath* [*ruah*], and breathe upon these slain, that they may live." I prophesied as he commanded me, and the *breath* [*ruah*] came into them, and they lived, and stood on their feet, a vast multitude. . . .

"I will put my *spirit* [*ruah*] within you, and you shall live, and I will place you upon your own soil; then you shall know that I, the LORD, have spoken and will act," says the LORD. (vv. 8–10, 14)

Oddly the NRSV renders *ruah* in verse 14 as "spirit." Within this imagery of restored Israel is a replication of the creation narrative in Genesis 2:7. Like Adam, Israel is scattered dirt, now breathed on and given a new future that, like the future of the world, depends on the *ruah* of YHWH, without which it reverts to the chaos of exile.

6. It is striking that in Psalm 51, the quintessential penitential psalm, the penitence is finished by verse 9. After that, the psalm is replete with hope-filled imperatives that expect God the creator to lift the psalmist from the vexation of guilt and alienation to the possibility of new life:

Create in me a clean heart, O God,
    and put a new and right spirit [*ruah*] within me.
Do not cast me away from your presence,
    and do not take your holy spirit [*ruah*] from me.
Restore to me the joy of your salvation,
    and sustain in me a willing spirit [*ruah*].

vv. 10–12

These lines are filled with hopeful, insistent petition, with *ruah* repeated three times. It is a bid for God's life-giving breath:

- Put a new and right *ruah* in me. "New" here is the same as in Psalm 104:30, "renew the ground." Both the ground and the person are new creations by and because of God's *ruah*.
- Take not your holy *ruah* from me, or else I will expire.
- Sustain in me a willing *ruah*.

The psalm goes on to praise and acknowledge that what God desires is a "broken *ruah*," a shattered sense of self-autonomy. The sum of these texts is glad dependence and a full recognition that life without God's *ruah* is impossible.

One last text, a seventh to round out the previous six: In John 20, after the initial discovery of the empty tomb (John 20:1–10) and after the appearance to Mary (vv. 11–18), Jesus comes to the disciples through locked doors (vv. 19–23). They were barricaded in fear, but he counters their fear: "Peace be with you." After they see his hands and side and rejoice, he reiterates, "Peace be with you." And then, says the narrator, "He breathed on them and said to them, 'Receive the Holy Spirit'" (v. 22).

Jesus gives them power to forgive, which links "spirit" and "forgive" in a way that recalls Psalm 51. Here Jesus does for the disciples, the new humanity, the new creation, what God does for humanity in Genesis 2:7 and for Israel in Ezekiel 37. As prehumanity was dust, so the prechurch was scattered in fearful dismay. The resurrection appearances showcase the creator God forming a new world and a new humanity with passion, vitality, and freedom, in order to do the things of God: justice, peace, forgiveness, reconciliation, and transformation. We only know how to speak of this new creation, of new *ruah*, because we have the rhetoric of creation, which tells of the *ruah*. Imagine, a world breathed on!

5. Creation and Righteous Judgment

The fourth and final theme is found in Psalm 104:35a. After the glorious wonders of the defeat of chaos (vv. 25–26), the generous guarantee of food (vv. 27–28), and the reliable gift of *ruah* (vv. 29–30), this verse comes as a great surprise, one we are scarcely prepared for:

> Let sinners be consumed from the earth,
>   and let the wicked be no more.

In a two-line parallel, this verse anticipates and wills the nullification of sinners and obliteration of the wicked. "Sinners" and "wicked" appear here for the first time in Psalm 104 and interrupt the wonder and awe of Israel before the goodness of the creator and creation. It is as though this verse, with these two malefactors, jerks us back into social reality after a fantasy of divine well-being. This verse is a jarring interruption that we often skip over.

But not so fast. This verse reminds us that creation is no free lunch. The verse draws our doxology back to the world of Israel's covenantal seriousness. "Sinners and the wicked" are those who violate and harm the community by their refusal to adhere to covenantal norms. Thus, the verse looks back to and echoes Psalm 1:4–5, which speaks of the commandments and uses the same word pair. Israel understood that participation in the life of God's generous creation is a two-way street. Creation is constituted by gifts but also commandments. The prophets are alert to the wonder of the large scope of creation, but they resolutely focus on the responsibility humans have to adhere to the limits, the choices, the givens, and the connections of creation that cannot be violated with impunity. If and when such violating takes place, consequences of curse come—in prophetic terms this is the judgment of God.

But we need not begin (or end) with the negative. Consider what righteousness looks like when faithfully practiced:

- Righteousness is glad acceptance that God the creator has decisively *defeated chaos*, and so righteousness is to live freely without anxiety.
- Righteousness is glad acceptance that God has *provided ample food* for all creatures, and so righteousness is to be willing to share without excessive accumulation.
- Righteousness is glad dependence on the *reliable ruah-giving God*, and so righteousness is to relinquish efforts at control and immortality by holding one's breath.

Righteousness, in sum, is glad acceptance of the good ordering of reality given and guaranteed by the creator, and culminating in Sabbath. Conversely, wickedness refuses that glad acceptance:

- Wickedness is to *assume the continuing force of chaos*, and so wickedness is to seek to amass whatever it takes—money, power, weapons, sex, and influence—to fend off chaos for one's own interests.
- Wickedness is to assume that there is no reliable supply of abundant bread, and so wickedness is to seek a *monopoly of bread* at the expense of the neighbor.
- Wickedness is to imagine that *ruah belongs to us* and not to God, and so wickedness is to practice hubris in order to maintain one's own life and place in the world.

Wickedness, in sum, is the refusal of God the creator and the idolization of self as the center of reality. No wonder sinners will be consumed and the wicked will be no more. Creation is a gift that keeps on giving. At the same time, it is a summons that keeps summoning to a decision for life or death, for the blessings promised in Genesis 1 or the curses that have quotidian specificity (see Deut. 28:15–19).

6. Back to Doxology

Psalm 104:35a is a sober but brief note that is surrounded by doxology. After the three themes of *the defeat of chaos* (vv. 25–26), *the supply of ample food* (vv. 27–28), and *the gift of ruah* (vv. 29–30), verses 31–34 voices a grand doxology interrupted for a brief moment by the worrisome but important fourth theme of verse 35a. Finally, the very end of the psalm (v. 35b) returns to verse 1: "Bless the LORD, O my *nephesh*," the very *nephesh* formed by *ruah* in Genesis 2:7. Note too that in 104:31–34, the psalm twice uses the term "rejoice":

> May YHWH rejoice. (v. 31)
> I will rejoice. (v. 34)

YHWH and I, YHWH and Israel, YHWH and creation together! The pivot of doxology in this psalm is found in verse 24, the second forceful naming of YHWH. In a word, Israel is simply stunned by creation. That stunning is not about a *doctrine* but about *the daily stuff* of our lives: grass, water, wine, oil, bread, moon, sun, darkness—the specificity of life given by the generosity of God.

It is all doxology, not argument, science, or even morality. It is the self-giving of Israel back to the overwhelming creator God. The praise sung here wills life back to the source and end of self, with nothing held back in reserve—not name, not property—but all yielded gladly.

Who should sing such praise?

> *I* will sing to the LORD . . .
> *I* will sing praise to my God.
> v. 33

The doxology begins (v. 1) and ends (v. 35) with "*O my soul.*" This "I" and "my" is intimate and personal, the fullness of the *nephesh* given back to God.

But the self is not alone; it is joined in praise by neighbors:

> Let those who desire my vindication
> shout for joy and be glad,
> and say evermore,
> "Great is the LORD,
> who delights in the welfare of his servant."
> Ps. 35:27; cf. 22:22, 25

Even that is not enough. The *self* and *neighbors* are joined by *others* who salute and trust in the creator:

> Praise him, sun and moon;
> praise him, all you shining stars!
> Praise him, you highest heavens,
> and you waters above the heavens! . . .
> Praise the LORD from the earth,
> you sea monsters and all deeps,
> fire and hail, snow and frost,
> stormy wind fulfilling his command!
> Mountains and all hills,
> fruit trees and all cedars!

> Wild animals and all cattle,
>   creeping things and flying birds!
> Ps. 148:3–4, 7–10

How long should this doxology continue? As long as one can imagine:

> as long as I live . . .
> while I have being.
> Ps. 104:33

All this praise is directed toward God:

- Praise to *the mighty Father* who defeated chaos.
- Praise to *the generous Son* who provided the heavenly banquet of the Eucharist.
- Praise to *the enlivening Spirit* who gives *ruah* to all creatures.

Alternatively, it is:

- Praise to Jesus who defeated the powers of chaos (Mark 4:35–41);
- Praise to Jesus who provided ample food (Mark 8:1–10);
- Praise to Jesus who breathed on us an Easter breath (John 20:22).

It is praise to God who gives, offered by us who receive.

This glad ceding of self in doxology is the evangelical antidote to the violation of the good creation caused by anxiety: violence, exploitation, commoditization, imperialism, oppression. The danger is always that our doxology stays on the surface, above the pathology. But Psalm 104 intends that this doxology go all the way down to the bottom of the depths and to the top of the dome, all over and everywhere. That's why the book of Psalms ends:

> Let everything that breathes [*neshamah*] praise the LORD!
> Praise the LORD!
> Ps. 150:6

Questions for Reflection

1. If you were to take an inventory of your life today, and frame it with a deep expansive doxology as in Psalm 104, what would you include in your prayer of praise to God? Think as the psalmist does, both generally, and in specifics.

2. As you consider chaotic forces active in our world today, how does the psalmist's doxological move of reframing chaos from world-devouring threat to just one of God's many works change your worldview?

3. What is your tradition of prayer at the table? How might it change with the idea that gratitude for daily bread, like the church's eucharistic table, is a defiant counter to the anxious scarcity so prevalent in our world?

4. Consider the ways Psalm 104 uses the Hebrew word *ruah*. What is your understanding of the connection between the gift of God's breath and the gift of God's spirit for you, for the church, and for all of creation as "a world breathed on"?

PART THREE

Lament and Complaint

Chapter 7

Cries That Seek God's Engagement

*C*hurch people who seriously engage the book of Psalms are often surprised, sometimes offended, to discover that much of the Psalter consists of abrasive truth-telling. Approximately one-third of the psalms voice laments/complaints/protests that disturb and challenge our conventional, comfortable notions of faith. We are surprised, if not offended, by these psalms because so much conventional prayer and worship are celebrative, affirmative, and buoyant; as a result we flinch to hear that often (not seldom) in the Psalms is heard "a discouraging word." But the voice in these lament psalms knows that life does not consist solely of matters to celebrate and affirm and that we are not always left buoyed by the realities of our lives.

In the book of Psalms we have to do, as the Episcopal prayer asserts, with the God from whom no secrets are hid. The lament psalms, in particular, are the telling of all our secrets to God—the hidden, dark, painful, needy secrets that we prefer not to have or acknowledge. The Psalter exhibits an awareness that well-being depends on such truth-telling that draws God into the negations of life in the insistent expectation that God can make something new of such negations.

The psalms of lament/complaint/protest no doubt grew out of specific circumstances in which persons *in extremis* voiced their extremity of need to God on the assumption that the *extremis* mattered to God. What was originally spontaneous prayer evoked by emergency has been shaped, through many repeated uses, into a highly stylized way of speaking so that subsequent practitioners of these prayers can replicate the original vitality of such utterance.

Four patterns of rhetoric are reiterated in the recurring, stylized speech of these psalms.

Complaint

After a summoning address to God that God should listen, the lament psalms present a *complaint* that voices to God the crisis situation that needs attention. The rhetorical strategy is to describe the speaker's plight in the most dire way, likely in order to get God's attention and to motivate God's engagement. The situation of dismay, which is often quite detailed, may be one of sickness, social isolation, and shame or, more publicly, a social crisis of drought or defeat in war. In every case, it is a circumstance in which the speaker lacks, in and of herself, resources to cope adequately with the crisis. The speaker is under assault and at risk before the power of death, which can take many forms:

> O LORD, how many are my foes!
>> Many are rising against me.
>>> Ps. 3:1

> I am weary with my moaning;
>> every night I flood my bed with tears;
>> I drench my couch with my weeping.
> My eyes waste away because of grief;
>> they grow weak because of all my foes.
>>> 6:6–7

> For the insolent have risen against me,
>> the ruthless seek my life;
>> they do not set God before them.
>>> 54:3

This is no-holds-barred truth-telling in which the intent is to make the circumstance of need as acute as can be imagined. Indeed, the rhetoric is a kind of brinkmanship that puts God on notice that the need is so great that if God does not do something—and soon—death will prevail. These prayers assume that this dramatic transaction presents to God what God does not know until it has been said aloud. They also assume that God is indeed on the other end of the transaction. This is real speech, not playacting!

Petition

On the basis of the complaint, the laments then center in on the *petition* that follows, which is an imperative asking God to notice, attend, and intervene. The assumption here is that if God can be moved to act, all will be well. The petition is in fact an act of great nerve, because the speaker dares to address an imperative to God. The force of the imperative is direct, like a command—the sort of command that violates normal protocol but that one might risk in a context of urgent need:

> Answer me when I call, O God of my right! . . .
> Be gracious to me, and hear my prayer.
> 4:1

> Be gracious to me, O LORD, for I am languishing;
> O LORD, heal me, for my bones are shaking with terror.
> 6:2

> Rise up, O LORD, in your anger;
> lift yourself up against the fury of my enemies;
> awake, O my God; you have appointed a judgment.
> 7:6

> Hear a just cause, O LORD; attend to my cry;
> give ear to my prayer from lips free of deceit. . . .
> Guard me as the apple of the eye;
> hide me in the shadow of your wings.
> 17:1, 8

These are no trivial or casual requests. They are urgings on which everything—life-or-death!—depends.

Such daring speech depends on two grounds. On the one hand, such urging arises from dire *social or bodily need*. It may or may not be grounded in theological conviction, but it certainly arises from the most elemental sense of jeopardy. On the other hand, such urging depends on the fact that Israel in its petition has a *sense of entitle-ment* before God. The Israelite is in covenant with God, and God has pledged attentive protection and sustenance. In the lament, Israel is calling on God to fulfill God's side of the covenantal agreement as a verification that God can be trusted to be faithful. This is not simple or merely some sort of self-talk, psychological activity, as we in our modern rationality often think prayer to be. This is a real transaction, raw, innocent, and trusting.

This raw innocence is evident in the candor of the petition. In one of the most problematic elements of the petition, the speaker often requests not only respite for one's self, which is legitimate enough in a covenantal context, but also, in addition to that, forceful action that God should take against the speaker's detractors and adversaries:

> Rise up, O LORD!
>   Deliver me, O my God!
> For you strike all my enemies on the cheek;
>   you break the teeth of the wicked.
>   3:7

> Break the arm of the wicked and evildoers;
>   seek out their wickedness until you find none.
> The LORD is king forever and ever;
>   the nations shall perish from his land.
>   10:15–16

> O God, break the teeth in their mouths,
>   tear out the fangs of the young lions, O LORD!
> Let them vanish like water that runs away;
>   like grass let them be trodden down and wither.
> Let them be like the snail that dissolves into slime;
>   like the untimely birth that never sees the sun.
> Sooner than your pots can feel the heat of thorns,
>   whether green or ablaze, may he sweep them away!
>   58:6–9

The speaker is able to get "down and dirty" in regressive, even childish speech about real feelings. But it is crucial to observe that in these prayers for violence against one's adversaries, it is not suggested that the petitioners themselves would or should enact such violence.

All that is left to God, and God, in God's freedom, will process the petition and act in God's own sovereign wisdom. That certitude permits Israel to voice its "heart's desire," ignoble as it may be and sometimes is. Whatever the case, Israel feels free to voice the deepest urge for retaliation and vengeance against those who diminish life. And God is regarded as an ally in the struggle for an undiminished life.

Reasons

As though to reinforce and accent the urgency of the petition, the psalms of lament often include a most interesting rhetorical motif: the speaker offers God *reasons* for answering the petition. It is almost as if God is thought to ask, in response to the petition, "Now why should I do *that*?" So the psalmist provides various answers to that question, each of which seeks to motivate God to act. These motivations tend to play on God's character and God's self-regard. For example, Psalm 86:1–2 includes the petitions: "incline . . . answer . . . preserve." The reasons that God should respond to these petitions are because of who God is:

> For you, O Lord, are good and forgiving,
> abounding in steadfast love to all who call on you.
> . . . .
> But you, O Lord, are a God merciful and gracious,
> slow to anger and abounding in steadfast love and faithfulness.
> 86:5, 15

It is as though God needs to be reminded that God is characterized in this way. God should act, in the case of this particular psalm, to verify that God is indeed the God of covenantal fidelity, as Israel has long confessed (see Exod. 34:6–7; Num. 14:18). The reasons seek to mobilize God's best self in a fidelity that is more than enough to overcome the situation of distress.

But in some psalms the motivation is not only about the character of God. It also concerns the predisposition of the speaker as a pious adherent to YHWH. Thus the petitions of Psalm 86:1–2 are followed by two particles, "for," that have the force of "because":

> *because* I am poor and needy;
> *because* I am devoted to you.

In these statements, the speaker combines both desperate need and covenantal devotion, both of which place God under some obligation. Thus the two reasons in verses 1–2, together with the motivations in verses 5 and 15, play both sides of the covenant: "God is merciful" meets "I am needy and devoted to God." The hope in this interface is for God's full enactment of covenantal fidelity that will bring well-being.

A more surprising motivation is to play on God's self-regard that runs toward divine vanity. God wants to be well thought of by other gods and by other peoples. It is assumed that God wants to be praised. In Psalm 35, the offer of praise to God is something of a bargaining chip. Praise is to be given to God when God acts, but it is withheld until God intervenes to rescue:

> Then my soul shall rejoice in the LORD,
>   exalting in his deliverance.
> All my bones shall say,
>   "O LORD, who is like you?"
> . . . .
> Then I will thank you in the great congregation;
>   in the mighty throng I will praise you.
> . . . .
> Then my tongue shall tell of your righteousness
>   and of your praise all day long.
>   vv. 9–10, 18, 28

The condition of praise is God's delivering action. When the action is completed and the speaker is rescued, then God will be praised— but not until then!

The same assumption about praise for God is evident in the challenging rhetorical questions of Psalm 88:

> Do you work wonders for the dead?
>   Do the shades rise up to praise you?
> Is your steadfast love declared in the grave,
>   or your faithfulness in Abaddon?
> Are your wonders known in the darkness,
>   or your saving help in the land of forgetfulness?
>   vv. 10–12

The implied answer to all these questions is no: no praise in death, no witness to divine miracles in the darkness of death. The implication is that if God wants to be praised (as God most certainly does), then God must keep the witnesses alive, which means they must be saved. It is in God's own self-interest to do so. The motivation for divine rescue is that God will receive the praise to which God is entitled and that God so much wants. Praise enhances God in the eyes of the other gods and the other peoples. The psalmist knows that and trades on it.

This sort of prayer may strike us as regressive, even childish somehow, unworthy of good worshipers and surely unworthy of the God of the Bible. But that is exactly the point. Honest prayer expresses the basest reality of our lives. It runs the risk of implying problems for God if praise is withheld. It assumes that one has leverage with God in prayer and that God can thereby be compelled to act in ways that God might otherwise not act. This kind of venturesome speech is not something we readily do when all is well. When all is well, we might even disapprove of people praying this way. But when life is not well and we are pushed to extremes, the lament psalms offer a model of engagement in full candor with the God of transformative possibility. Such prayer is intense, dangerous, and urgent. It moves deeply beneath our usual innocuous prayer in which nothing is at stake, because in this kind of prayer everything is at stake.

Resolution

These prayers of complaint are, in the final analysis, acts of hope. They believe and assume that the present circumstances of trouble will not endure. These speakers expect God to change such circumstances and believe they are entitled to such change. This is why, with only two exceptions, Psalms 39 and 88, these prayers regularly end in *positive resolution*. By the end of the psalm, we are assured that God has heard, and God has acted, and well-being has been restored. Thus the prayers culminate in exuberant affirmation and praise, because the daring prayers of Israel have evoked the life-giving power of God:

I cry aloud to the LORD,
and he answers me from his holy hill.
3:4

You have put gladness in my heart
more than when their grain and wine abound.
I will both lie down and sleep in peace;
for you alone, O LORD, make me lie down in safety.
4:7–8

The LORD has heard my supplication;
the LORD accepts my prayer.
6:9

O LORD, you will hear the desire of the meek;
you will strengthen their heart, you will incline your ear.
10:17

By the end of the prayer, covenantal equilibrium will have been reestablished!

This remarkable pattern of lament is a shock to many because traditional Christian prayer is far more polite and deferential. It does not crowd God but waits patiently for God's good mercy. But there is nothing polite or deferential about much of lament prayer. Rather, these lament prayers specialize in self-announcement that refuses patient waiting. To be sure, such a posture is provisional. If it were more than provisional, it would amount to hubris. By the end of the laments, then, when covenantal equilibrium is reestablished, there is a return to the "normal" practice of praise and thanks. Even so, these prayers know that descent into demanding candor is essential for life in the world and for life before God.

Lament prayer seems odd to us, because the church has, for the most part, refused such prayer. The result of that refusal is that much contemporary prayer is denial, as though our secrets can be hid from God. But they cannot. We see continuing traces of that raw dialogic practice of lament prayer, here and there, now and then—for example, 12-step programs or in the "stages of grief" that are now so popular. For the most part, however, these contemporary practices are either thoroughly secularized or reduced to "mere" psychology.

While we should be glad for the lingering residue of Israel's lament, we should, even more than that, be grateful for these scripts and models of prayer that stake everything on full covenantal honesty in the presence of God. Such daring honesty, at God's throne of mercy, is the only route to transformative well-being. That is the secret of the laments that cannot be hid.

Questions for Reflection

1. With the model of the Psalms' abrasive truth-telling, what specifics of complaint are in your cry to God today, or have been in the past? Consider situations in which you have found yourself without the resources to cope on your own.

2. What were you taught about the appropriate language of prayer? How naturally does the daring speech of petition, in which dire need and covenantal entitlement are freely shared with a trustworthy God, come to you?

3. Lament psalms, which make up one-third of the Psalter, stand in contrast with our "usual innocuous prayer in which nothing is at stake." How often do your own prayers—or those of your worshiping community—include the kind of truth-telling modeled in these psalms?

4. Lament prayers are "acts of hope" that expect resolution. Which of the verses noted in this chapter can serve as a script for your own prayers the next time you find yourself in need of a daring, honest, and hopeful cry to God?

Chapter 8

The Formfulness of Grief

*T*he lament psalms offer important resources for Christian faith and ministry, even though they have been largely purged from the life of the church and its liturgical use. Such purging attests to the alienation between the Bible and the church. This chapter seeks to consider ways in which the lament psalms might be appropriated for the life and faith of the church.[1]

I

Scholarship on the literary, rhetorical, and formal features of Israel's laments is fairly settled.[2] Questions about their setting in Israel's social life, however, are less clear. Many have assumed that the lament form for the individual has an institutional placement in a judicial process in the Jerusalem temple.[3] The lament form is used in the central shrine for an encounter concerning safety, innocence, acquittal, and well-being of the suppliant. Several studies have moved beyond this consensus and shifted attention from form and setting to function:

Editor's note: The increased engagement with secondary literature in this chapter is a consequence of the context in which these ideas initially appeared, a journal read primarily by people with formal training in biblical scholarship. More than forty years on, the tension between formalism and antiformalism, or what this chapter calls formfulness versus formlessness, remains a significant matter of contention among highly influential thinkers in the humanities and social sciences.

1. Claus Westermann has shown that the central movement of the lament is a sharp, discontinuous step from plea to praise, from brokenness to wholeness, even as he largely follows Joachim Begrich's hypothesis that a priestly authority likely uttered a "salvation oracle" in this interval between plea and praise. Westermann stresses the function of the form, that is, the way Israel was restored to full life and affirmative faith.[4]

2. Erhard Gerstenberger (a) has challenged the Jerusalem setting and has situated the form in the context of tribe or clan, and (b) has shown that its function is *rehabilitation* of a member to the lifeworld of the group.[5] The form serves the function of rehabilitation.

3. Rainer Albertz has made a shrewd distinction: (a) traditions of the creation of the world have their setting in the official cult of the great sanctuary and are expressed as hymns; (b) traditions of the creation of humans have their setting in the worship of small groups subordinate to official religion and are expressed in laments. As mentioned earlier, Albertz uses the term "cult" to refer to the religious system's *care* for the deity, which is the meaning of the Latin root *cultus*, and so should be understood in the sense of cultivated veneration rather than some sort of unorthodox sect. The purpose of the lament therefore differs from the hymn; the lament aims to create and restore the member of the community by the action of the group. Again the function is *rehabilitation/restoration*, and the form serves that function.[6]

In considering the interaction of form and function, we are helped by sociologists who see regularized language as the way a community creates and maintains a lifeworld.[7] Such regularized speech activity serves both to *enhance* the experience so that dimensions of it are not lost and to *limit* the experience so that some dimensions are denied their legitimacy. This suggests, applied to the lament form, that its regularized use intends to enable and require "sufferers" in the community to experience their suffering in a legitimate lifeworld. It is this form that *enhances* experience and brings it to articulation and also *limits* the experience of suffering so that it can be received and coped with according to the perspectives, perceptions, and resources of the community. Thus the function of the form is definitional. It tells the experiencer the shape of the experience that is legitimate to be experienced.

All the uses of this form in Israel or elsewhere insist that grief is formful. It can be supervised according to community forms that make it bearable and manageable in the community. The griever is kept in community or returned to the community by having it articulated that this experience does not lie outside the legitimate scope of the community. It is not an abyss—either anomic or chaotic.[8] By the use of the lament form the grief experience is made bearable and, it is hoped, meaningful. The form makes the experience formful just when it appeared to be formless and therefore deathly and destructive.

Granted the common characteristics, the lament form has different nuances when used in Israel: (a) as Begrich has noted, in Israel there is no attempt to flatter the deity, as there was in Babylon; (b) an affirmative ending is characteristic in Israel;[9] (c) the God of Israel's laments may enter the pathos with Israel.[10] These distinctive nuances are linguistic acts by which this community insists on a specific and distinctive formfulness that defines grief in a different way and makes it an altogether different experience. *Form permits the community to have a different experience*: (a) no flattery means that YHWH can be confronted directly and with bold confidence;[11] (b) the affirmative ending shows it is a believable complaint, focused on fidelity and not primarily on anger. To address YHWH, even in anger, is to make an affirmation about YHWH's character; Gerstenberger has distinguished lament (*Klage*) from complaint (*Anklage*) to suggest that Israel characteristically complains and does not lament—that is, it expects something.[12] Israel hopes for an intrusion that will fulfill the petition.[13] Finally, (c) the pathos of God in response to the trouble of the speaker is a theme not yet seriously explored; God's response indicates God's involvement and so makes an important assertion about the character of YHWH:

> The lament of the nation contains a dimension of protest. . . . It is a protest directed to God to be sure, but it is nevertheless a protest; it does not endure absurdity submissively and patiently: it protests! . . . It lays the matter out before God so that he will do something about it.[14]

The function of the form is (a) to give a new definition of the situation, and (b) to get some action that is hoped for because of this peculiar definitional world. The lament form not only describes what is but articulates what is expected and insisted upon.

II

To explore this form and function further, we will consider a contemporary attempt to characterize the formfulness of grief from the work of Elisabeth Kübler-Ross.[15] As is well known, Kübler-Ross has observed (and urged) that the grief and death process tends to follow a fairly regular form. That discernment on her part is a remarkable achievement. Technical medicine, like urban consciousness generally, is resistant to form, denies the formfulness of experience, and resists the notion that grief or any other experience is formful. Thus it is important that Kübler-Ross has been able to establish the agenda that this human experience is inevitably *formful*, and no technical claim to the contrary can deny that. The conflict between *formfulness* and the ideology of *formlessness* of experience in urban consciousness is a more urgent matter for form critics than we have often recognized.[16] The issues of form are urgently current and not only of historical interest. I consider this more important than the specifics of Kübler-Ross's work. The death-grief process includes five elements, according to Kübler-Ross:

1. *Denial and isolation*: "No, not me, it cannot be true."[17] Such denials lead to immobilizing isolation. This is a brief and temporary period.
2. *Anger*: Kübler-Ross reports the deep humiliation and indignity at being at the disposal of others, of being victimized by institutional routines, of not being important and having to wait, of being object rather than subject. A competent "I" is reduced to a worthless "it."
3. *Bargaining*: This is an attempt to postpone, to get parole for good behavior, usually related to religion or virtue. They are attempts to reduce life to quid pro quo. There is no bargaining power and not much is to be gained because there is no *quid*.
4. *Depression*: This occurs when the deep encompassing sense of loss hits the sufferer. It is the sense of nothingness that makes

one powerfully aware of lost opportunities, weakness, and the inability to function as a provider. The final insight is the worthlessness of it all.

5. *Acceptance*: The patient accepts the radical, ultimate loss. It is a mood in which the fighting ceases. It is not chagrinned resignation but an affirmation of the "all-rightness" of what is going on. It is a *surrender* of self-sufficiency, but it is also *reconciliation*. It is cessation of attempts at self-security and self-justification and an affirmation of the coherence and settledness of life in a context of larger meanings. In this stage, says Kübler-Ross, hope is strong, not grounded in medical possibilities, but in a sense of buoyancy about the reliable context in which life is lived and given up.

Kübler-Ross's five elements can be correlated with the movement in Israel's laments discerned by Westermann. She has discerned four stages that speak of *plea* and one that speaks of *affirmation*.[18] There is a radical turn between numbers 4 and 5 above, a turn as radical as that noted by Begrich and Westermann regarding Israel's lament psalms. Israel and Kübler-Ross begin at very different places, yet evidence striking similarities. (In my comparison I will work from Kübler-Ross's simpler form.)

III

1. *Denial*. In a modern technological hospital organized to deny reality,[19] the form begins with a predictable denial, not only by persons but by the definitional world of the medical community. Israel's form has no precise counterpart because Israel's speech begins with an insistent covenantal address, identifying one who is expected to be present. The contrasting moods are the *resignation* of aloneness and the *protest* of covenantal relatedness. Israel's speech presumes a history of interaction, of speaking and hearing that gives life. In the urban consciousness, loss must be faced without history, and so, instead of covenantal address, there is denial.

2. *Anger*. Kübler-Ross's second stage offers a central parallel. Israel asserts indignation at being cheated, exploited, humiliated,

betrayed, and abandoned. It articulates rage against all comers, as does Kübler-Ross's form. Because of covenant, Israel had a context in which this could be received and contained, whereas Kübler-Ross observed that family and staff cannot cope with it.[20] The modern context lacks the resources to contain and receive such undisciplined, irrational assertions, because death as well as life is supposed to be much more managed and buttoned down. While the forms contain the same elements in Israel, the covenantal form can embrace the primordial sense of irrationality and does not need to be reduced to scientific rationality.

3. *Bargaining.* This is a minor motif for Kübler-Ross, as it has been for form studies of Israel's lament. But, in both cases, the motif is the same. As for Kübler-Ross, Israel's reasons include good behavior, trust, faithfulness, and innocence. The Israelites are much bolder and more inventive because they are not constrained to be polite. To motivate God to act, they resort to threats, intimidation, and appeals to YHWH's pride and vanity. In both forms, the bargaining is a last, desperate attempt at self-sufficiency and self-justification (this is clearest in the protests of Job).

4. *Depression.* Kübler-Ross means by this a sense of worthlessness, impotence, and insignificance, as well as the behavior derived from it. That motif is hinted at in Israel through expressions of bitter helplessness:

> But I am a worm, and not human;
>   scorned by others, and despised by the people.
> All who see me mock at me;
>   they make mouths at me, they shake their heads.
>   Ps. 22:6–7

Such speech concerns being at the disposal of another who does not seem to care or value the sufferer (6:6–7; 13:1–2; on the "worm" theme, see also Job 25:6). Israel knows about that sense of diminishment and self-deprecation, but it is differently textured. Kübler-Ross's subject has no one to address and so will finally be depressed. Israel, always by form, has a partner to whom to speak. For that reason, Israel's anger is much more healthy and buoyant. It is fundamentally hopeful, because there is always a chance that the other one will act.[21] Depression is never full-blown in Israel, because there is in the form another one who listens and takes Israel's speech seriously. In place of depression, Israel's form has petition, and here the forms are most to be contrasted. Depression is appropriate if the speech is finally monologic. But Israel's form is boldly dialogic, and the one who hears, or is expected to hear, is not addressed in hopeless despair but in passionate expectation.[22]

5. *Acceptance*. Kübler-Ross's fifth stage correlates to Begrich's idea that the psalmist moves from lament to praise after hearing a religious authority utter a salvation oracle in which God promises to deliver the petitioner from their distress. The decisive turn in the form is the same. For Kübler-Ross, it is the turn between elements number 4 and 5, and for Israel the turn from petition to praise. In both, there is a dramatic movement toward affirmation and readiness to rejoice. It is unclear, concerning Kübler-Ross, whether "acceptance" is affirmation or whether it is resignation. I believe she herself is not clear.

While the modern resolution may or may not be affirmative, Israel's conclusion is characteristically praise. The doxology rests on the conviction that the griever has been heard and the matter has been dealt with decisively.

IV

Again assuming Begrich's hypothesis that the movement to praise is accomplished by faithful speaking, precisely by the one who seems absent or unconcerned, then the situation is changed not by a visible action, not by external transformation, but by a word spoken authoritatively. This word constructs and maintains a social reality that in the distress seemed to have slipped away or collapsed. It is the function of the form to assert the power and credibility of the words of this community, words that assert and express a reality only this community knows about and that are decisively powerful there. These words dramatize the claim of the entire form, namely, that grief and loss are not formless but formful. Their form is dialogic and not monologic.

In a much more timid way, Kübler-Ross makes the same point. The speech that moves the dying one to acceptance is not the authoritative "Fear not, I am with you," as in Israel's form, but the form is similarly employed:

CHAPLAIN: A certain sense of dignity she'd want to maintain as long as she could.

PATIENT: Yes, and I can't do this alone at times.[23]

Kübler-Ross writes: "In the preparatory grief there is no or little need for words. It is much more a feeling that can be mutually expressed and is often done better with a touch of a hand, a stroking of the hair, or just a silent sitting together" (Kübler-Ross, *On Death and Dying*, 87; see 106, 110). Kübler-Ross makes two summary statements:

> We have found that those patients do best who have been encouraged to express their rage, to cry in preparatory grief, and to express their fears and fantasies to someone who can sit quietly and listen. (Kübler-Ross, *On Death and Dying*, 119)

> Our presence may just confirm that we are going to be around until the end. (113)

Mutatis mutandis, these are all variations on "Fear not, I am with you." As in Israel, the form affirms faithful speaking and not technical medicine or jargon. With Israel, it is the word of YHWH. With Kübler-Ross, it is the voice of human folk who will not be denied their human function by a technical institution that finally can neither give life nor prevent others from that function.

The form moves from "Fear not, I am with you," to "I will not fear, for you are with me" (Ps. 23:4). It is the function of the form (and nothing else will do it) to deal with the elemental, even primordial, fear of anomie, chaos, death, and abandonment. The problem of the situation may indeed be sickness, enemies, or death. But such experiences finally concern formlessness, the collapse of categories in which experience can be experienced in a universe of meaning. In Israel, the formfulness of the experience centers in the presence of YHWH, who need not do anything but be there. The use of the form is an activity in the maintenance of this lifeworld that has at its center the abiding, transforming presence of YHWH.[24] No less so in Kübler-Ross, this form that requires a dialogue partner between numbers 4 and 5 is a form that technical medicine does not understand, surely does not sanction, but can neither prevent nor displace. This form also is a response to the yearning for assurance that the experience is not formless, that there is something that endures outside the experience of loss. That enduring reality is a faithful word.

The commonalities in the forms of Israel and Kübler-Ross are instructive. Most important of course is the movement in each from negation to affirmation. The movement of both these forms cannot be made by the sufferer alone but depends on the presence of a voice that has history with the subject.

The *dissimilarities* are all the more striking: (a) Israel practices covenantal address instead of denial; (b) Israel engages in expectant petition instead of depression; (c) in Israel, the form itself centers in intervention, whereas Kübler-Ross must treat the intervention ambiguously and gingerly because the context of modernity must by definition screen it out; and (d) in Israel, the form of the rhetoric, like the form of the event, is undeniably covenantal. As such, the form serves to set the experience of grief and suffering in a context of covenant, which means that expected transforming intrusion by the covenant partner is a legitimate and intentional extrapolation from the form itself.[25] This of course Kübler-Ross has not found in the parallel form and cannot. Modernity cannot anticipate a "breakthrough."

V

Because Kübler-Ross has so captured the imagination of caring people, it is appropriate to comment on her work in light of Israel's laments:

1. The form she presents is a yearning for covenant rather than an affirmation of it, which may be the most that can be articulated in the world of urban consciousness.
2. The nature of the responding partner in her form—that is, a friend, relative, medical personnel—means that the move to the

affirmation is not full and buoyant, because such responding agents cannot powerfully intrude to transform. The formfulness of the event is essentially and necessarily humanistic. What is lacking is the presence of a sovereign God who can authorize.

3. Kübler-Ross appears to be ambivalent on the last stage of acceptance. At times, this appears to be triumphantly affirmative and at other times serenely resigned. It is not clear if we have a resigned lament or an expectant complaint. Such a lack of convinced clarity diminishes the power of the form.

4. Kübler-Ross may well be bootlegging a view of death that does not rely on the form but seeks to go outside and beyond it.[26] Thus death is not defeated as the last enemy but is embraced as the last home or, perhaps, as the last growth point. The easy alliance of biblical theology with her view in popular practice must be doubted. The form as she has presented it is less amenable to the biblical form if the latter is powerfully covenantal. The modern counterpart is not clearly covenantal and therefore cannot really be over against an enemy as it is in Israel's form.

5. Roy Branson has also suggested that Kübler-Ross at times is not descriptive. She urges acceptance of death with serenity. To the extent that this is true, the form she presents is quite at variance with Israel's perception of death as a conquered enemy. The fundamental conflict myth of Israel[27] has thus been dissipated into a stoic acceptance rather than a historical affirmation. The form discerned by Kübler-Ross has become an ideology that may serve well the interests of a death-denying production/consumption society.

6. Her more recent writing suggests that Kübler-Ross is not satisfied, unlike ancient Israel, with the discerned form and has moved far beyond the form to "religious" resolutions by researching patients who have "come back from death." Yet Israel also grew curious and inventive when the forms no longer seemed to accommodate the extremity of experience.

VI

None of this is intended as a critique of Kübler-Ross, for that is not the point of the discussion. Rather it is a way of discerning Israel's reliance on form.

1. Israel affirmed covenant as the enduring context for grief and loss.[28]
2. The responding partner is authoritatively YHWH. This is evident because of the "assurance of being heard," quite apart from Begrich's hypothesis. Death is dealt with in relation to the sovereignty and fidelity of YHWH.
3. The tone is triumphant at the end. It is not resignation or acceptance but praise addressed to one who has made a difference. A decision has been made that alters Israel's situation.
4. Israel has, by the form, decided about loss, grief, and death. They are real, and they are dangerous; but YHWH deals with them. That statement is powerful and valid in Israel's lifeworld. Outside of that lifeworld, the claim has no power or credibility.
5. This community form is neither descriptive nor prescriptive. It is a form in movement, task-oriented to rehabilitate members to a lifeworld in which transforming intervention is a live option.
6. The form is sufficient for Israel. No speculative probing beyond the form is needed. Perhaps later hints about resurrection in the apocalyptic literature may parallel Kübler-Ross's recent work, a grasping for assurance when the forms no longer carry the load.[29] The correlation between apocalyptic inventiveness and Kübler-Ross's subsequent speculation may point to the crisis in both communities—Israel's and ours—when form collapses or loses credibility. Such a collapse of form may also be indicated by the pervasive, contemporary quest for formless religious experience.

Such a contrast should urge persons charged with primarily theological offices to avoid settling completely for the frames of reference of the psychological disciplines that are insensitive to form and tend to be supportive of the ideology of urban consciousness.

In summary, then, the function of this lament form includes the following:

1. In the use of the form, the community does a specific task that is rehabilitation of a member from a chaotic experience to a structured experience in this particular lifeworld.
2. The use of the form serves to maintain and reassert the lifeworld of Israel as a valid symbolic context in which experience can be healingly experienced. While the form is surely liturgic

in some sense, it is also to be understood sociologically. The community asserts that *life in all its parts is formful and therefore meaningful.* Attention to language is crucial for a community's certainty of meaning.

3. The function of the form is inevitably theological. It constructs and presents a covenantal view of reality in which life is characterized by faithful hearing and speaking. The form itself defines theological reality. Such a conclusion is strengthened by Begrich's hypothesis that the psalmist received an oracle of salvation after the lament, but does not depend on it, for the "assurance of being heard" indicates that the speaking has been responded to in ways that matter.

4. This form, with its societal power, is likely not simply one form in a vast repertoire but is one of the constitutive forms of biblical faith.[30] It affirms that the holy God is moved by such address, is covenantally responsive to covenant claims, and that Israel lives by this God's transforming word. YHWH is not an apathetic God who either is silent or must be flattered.

5. Form critics might appropriately consider their work not simply as a part of historical research but as a major issue in the formlessness and antiform mentality of urban technological consciousness. The possibility of formfulness endures as a central question for us. Such formfulness will not be found in universal myths but in communities that have asserted their historical specificity. Perhaps it is the task of the theological community to recover confidence in historical specificity, which is a precondition to speech and therefore to liberation.[31]

Questions for Reflection

1. What are the ways in which the experience of grief has been "formful" within your family or faith community? In other words, what are your community's forms of grief that help redefine and point beyond the current situation? What language, experiences, and rituals have served the function of making grief bearable and, hopefully, meaningful?

2. Has your personal experience with grief followed the stages Kübler-Ross describes: denial, anger, bargaining, depression, acceptance?

However you have experienced grief, what helped you move from the stages that resemble "plea" to the last one of "affirmation"?

3. Brueggemann says that depression is never full-blown in the anger, grief, and lament of Israel because the bold, dialogical form assumes that God is listening and may act. In place of depression, the form of lament calls for petition in the context of a covenantal relationship. How does the conviction of having a listener on the other end of your prayers change your experience in the midst of lament and grief?

4. Brueggemann observes that "Israel has, by the form [of lament], decided about loss, grief, and death. They are real, and they are dangerous, but YHWH deals with them." How does the gospel of Jesus Christ inform this conclusion for the people of God and for you personally?

Chapter 9

The Costly Loss of Lament

Recent study of the lament psalms has indicated their enormous theological significance in the faith and liturgy of Israel and in their subsequent use by the church. There is no doubt that the lament psalms had an important function in the community of faith. In this chapter, I will explore the loss incurred when the lament psalms are no longer used for their specific social function in the church.

I

We may begin with a summary of the current scholarly consensus. Claus Westermann has done the most to help our understanding of the Psalms, and his work is surely normative for all other discussions.[1] Indeed, his work now has importance that ranks with that of Hermann Gunkel and Sigmund Mowinckel for our understanding of this literature.[2]

1. First, Westermann has shown that these psalms move from plea to praise.[3] In that move the situation and/or attitude of the speaker is transformed, and God is mobilized for the sake of the speaker. The intervention of God in some way permits the move from plea to praise.[4]

Editor's note: The increased engagement with secondary literature in this chapter is a consequence of the context in which these ideas initially appeared, a journal read primarily by people with formal training in biblical scholarship.

137

Second, Westermann has shown that the lament is resolved by and corresponds to the song of thanksgiving.[5] Indeed, the song of thanksgiving is in fact the lament restated after the crisis has been resolved. Westermann inclines to read this correspondence of lament and thanks as a subdued, regimented, and calculated form of response, whereas praise, in contrast with thanksgiving, is unfettered.[6]

Third, whatever one thinks of the contrast of thanksgiving and praise, Westermann has shown how the lament characteristically ends in praise that is full and unfettered. Indeed, the proper setting of praise is as lament resolved. In a sense, doxology and praise are best understood as responses to God's salvific intervention, which in turn is evoked by the lament.[7]

Fourth, Westermann himself has largely begged the question of life-setting—how psalms were used originally and in what contexts—for the laments. He is most reluctant to use the category of cult in the sense of ancient Israel's religious system, and when that category is denied, it is difficult to discuss institutional setting in any formal sense.[8]

Lastly, Westermann has not explicitly articulated the relational dynamics that go along with the structural elements. But I think it is safe to deduce from his form-critical analysis the following relational dynamic. In these psalms, Israel moves from *articulation* of hurt and anger, to *submission* of them to God, and finally *relinquishment*.[9] Functionally and experientially, the verbal articulation and the faithful submission to God are prerequisites for relinquishment. Only with such relinquishment can there be praise and acts of generosity. Thus the relational dynamic vis-à-vis God corresponds to the move of the formal elements.

2. The question of the setting in life of the lament psalms is not as clear as our understanding of the genre, perhaps because Westermann has not directly turned his attention to the issue. We may consider four elements of the scholarly discussion of this matter.

First, Mowinckel's temple hypothesis has largely dominated the discussion, and Aubrey Johnson has put the hypothesis to good use.[10] However, such a mode of interpretation has caused a sense of unreality about the laments, as though they are used as playacting in some great national drama, rather than the serious experience of members of the community.

Second, the language of the lament psalms reflects a juridical concern, which has led some to argue that the laments functioned primarily within juridical processes.[11] However, it is difficult to know how realistically to take the language. The hypothesis has suffered from an inclination to treat juridical language as only imitative. But in Psalm 109, for example, the appeal for a judge seems realistic, and the prayer petition is a request that the actual juridical procedure should be handled in a certain way.[12]

Third, the influential hypothesis of Mowinckel that the "evildoers" are people who work by sympathetic magic seems to me to be quite wrongheaded.[13] A more realistic sense of social process would indicate that those who are powerful enough to speak such words are the ones who administer, control, and benefit from social operations. This hypothesis again attempts to distance the laments from actual social processes, and thus reflects idealistic readings of the text.

Fourth, the work of Rainer Albertz and Erhard Gerstenberger seems to me to be most helpful in seeing that the laments are genuine pastoral activities.[14] Albertz has seen that the personal laments function in a *Kleinkult*, a more intimate and familial setting of religious life, apart from the temple and where the personal life-cycle processes of birth and death are in crisis. Gerstenberger has supported such a general sense of setting by placing these psalms in something like a house church or a base community in which members of the community enact a ritual of rehabilitation as an act of hope. This hypothesis has great plausibility and relates the poetry to real-life situations.

3. It is still the case that, even in the light of Westermann's great contribution, scholars have only minimally considered the theological significance of the lament psalm. We have yet to ask what it means to have this form available in this social construction of reality.[15] What difference does it make to have faith that permits and requires this form of prayer? My answer is that it shifts the calculus and *redresses the distribution of power* between the two parties, so that the petitionary party is taken seriously and the God who is addressed is newly engaged in the crisis in a way that puts God at risk. As the lesser, petitionary party (the psalm speaker) is legitimated, so the unmitigated supremacy of the greater party (God) is questioned, and God is made available to the petitioner. The basis for

the conclusion that the petitioner is taken seriously and legitimately granted power in the relation is that the speech of the petitioner is heard, valued, and transmitted as serious speech. Cultically, we may assume that such speech is taken seriously by God. One consequence of such a speech pattern and social usage is that it keeps all power relations under review and capable of redefinition.

The lament form thus concerns a redistribution of power. In what follows, I want to explore the negative implications of the redress of power. That is, I want to explore the questions: What happens when appreciation of the lament as a form of speech and faith is lost, as I think it is largely lost in contemporary usage? What happens when the speech forms that redress power distribution have been silenced and eliminated? The answer, I believe, is that a theological monopoly is reinforced, docility and submissiveness are engendered, and the outcome in terms of social practice is to reinforce and consolidate the political-economic monopoly of the status quo. In other words, the removal of lament from life and liturgy is not disinterested and, I suggest, only partly unintentional. In the following, I will explore two dimensions of the loss of lament and therefore two possible gains for the recovery of lament.

II

One loss that results from the absence of lament is the loss of *genuine covenant interaction*, since the second party to the covenant (the petitioner) has become voiceless or has a voice that is permitted to speak only praise and doxology. Where lament is absent, covenant comes into being only as a celebration of joy and well-being. Or in political categories, the greater party is surrounded by subjects who are always "yes-people" from whom "never is heard a discouraging word." Since such a celebrative, consenting silence does not square with reality, covenant minus lament is finally a practice of denial, cover-up, and pretense, which sanctions social control.

There is important heuristic gain in relating this matter to the theory of personality development called "object-relations theory."[16] The nomenclature is curious and misleading. The theory is a protest against psychological theories that claim that crucial matters of personality formation are internal to the person. Object-relations theory maintains instead that they are relational and external. "Object-relations" means that the person is related to real, objective others who are not a projection but are unyielding centers of power and will. For the very young child, one such objective other is, paradigmatically, the mother. For our subject, then, we can draw a parallel between child relating to mother and worshiper relating to God.

This theory argues that the child, if they are to develop ego-strength, must have initiative with the mother and an experience of omnipotence. This happens only if the mother is responsive to the child's gestures and does not take excessive initiative toward the child. Winnicott writes:

> A true self begins to have life through the strength given to the infant's weak ego by the mother's implementation of the infant's omnipotent expressions.[17]

The negative alternative is that the mother does not respond but takes initiative, and then the mother is experienced by the child as omnipotent:

> The mother who is not good enough is not able to implement the infant's omnipotence and so she repeatedly fails to meet the infant gesture. Instead she substitutes her own gesture which is to be given compliance by the infant. This compliance on the part of the infant is the earliest stage of the False Self, and belongs to the mother's inability to sense her infant's needs.[18]

We can draw a suggestive analogy from this understanding of the infant/mother relationship for our study of the lament. Where there is lament, the believer is able to take initiative with God and so develop over against God the ego-strength that is necessary for responsible faith. But where the capacity to initiate lament is absent, one is left only with praise and doxology. God then is omnipotent, always to be praised. The believer is nothing, and can praise or accept guilt uncritically where life with God does not function properly. The outcome is a "False Self," bad faith that is based in fear and guilt and lived out as resentful or self-deceptive works of righteousness. The absence of lament makes a religion of coercive obedience the only possibility.

I do not suggest that biblical faith be reduced to psychological categories, but I find this parallel suggestive. It suggests that the God who evokes and responds to lament is neither omnipotent in any conventional sense nor surrounded by docile reactors. Rather, this God is like a mother who dreams with this infant, that the infant may someday grow into a responsible, mature covenant partner who can enter into serious communion and conversation. In such a serious conversation and communion, there comes genuine obedience, which is not a contrived need to please, but a genuine, yielding commitment.

Where there is no lament through which the believer takes initiative, God is experienced like an omnipotent mother. What is left for the believer then is a false narcissism that keeps hoping for a centered self but lacks the ego-strength for a real self to emerge. What is at issue here, as Calvin understood so well, is a true understanding of the human self but, at the same time, a radical discernment of this God who is capable of and willing to be respondent and not only initiator.[19]

III

The second loss caused by the absence of lament is the *stifling of the question of theodicy*. I do not refer to some esoteric question of God's coping with ontological evil. Rather, I mean the capacity to raise legitimate questions of justice in terms of social goods, social access, and social power.[20] My sense is that, with regard to "theodicy," Israel is more concerned with *dikē* than with *theos*, more committed to questions of *justice* than to questions of *God*.[21] Thus the juridical hypotheses mentioned above are correct in seeing that the lament partakes of something of a claim filed in court in order to ensure that the question of justice is formally articulated.[22]

The lament psalms, then, are a complaint that makes the shrill insistence of the following:

- Things are not right in the present arrangement.
- They need not stay this way and can be changed.
- The speaker will not accept them in this way, for the present arrangement is intolerable.
- It is God's obligation to change things.[23]

The main point is the first: life is not right. It is now noticed and voiced that life is not as it was promised to be. The utterance of this awareness is an exceedingly dangerous moment at the throne. It is as dangerous as Lech Wałesa or Rosa Parks asserting with their bodies that the system has broken down and will no longer be honored. For the managers of the system—political, economic, religious, moral— there is always a hope that the troubled folks will not notice the dysfunction or that a tolerance of a certain degree of dysfunction can be accepted as normal and necessary, even if unpleasant. Lament occurs when the dysfunction reaches an unacceptable level, when the injustice is intolerable and change is insisted upon.

The lament/complaint can then go in two different directions. For each direction, I shall cite an extreme case. On the one hand, the complaint can be *addressed to God against neighbor*. Psalm 109 is an extreme case. The psalm is an appeal to the *hesed* (steadfast love) of YHWH (vv. 21, 26) against the failed *hesed* of the human agent (v. 16). God is a court of appeal through which a "better" juridical process is sought (see v. 6). Whereas human justice has failed, it is sure that God's justice is reliable. But notice that the plea concerns actual, concrete issues of justice, presumably having to do with property.

On the other hand, the complaint can be *addressed to God against God*. Psalm 88 is an extreme case. Here it is the justice of God that has failed. In such a case, Israel has no other court of appeal, and so, with great risk, Israel must return again and again to the same court with the same charge.[24] The psalm is relentless, and that must be reckoned a very dangerous act, to keep petitioning the court of YHWH against its own injustice. In both complaints, concerning failed human *hesed* and unresponsive God, the issue is justice. In each instance, the petitioner accepts no guilt or responsibility for the dysfunction but holds the other party responsible.

To be sure, these laments/complaints articulate a religious problem. But these speeches are not mere religious exercises, as though their value were principally cathartic. Rather, the religious speech always carries with it a surplus of political, economic, and social freight. The God addressed is either the legitimator and the guarantor of the social process (as in Ps. 88) or the court of appeal against the system (as in Ps. 109). The claims and rights of the speaker are asserted to God in the face of a system that does not deliver. That system is visible on earth and addressed in heaven with the passionate conviction that it can, must, and will be changed.

In regularly using the lament form, Israel kept the justice question visible and legitimate. It is this justice question in the form of lament that energizes the exodus narrative. Indeed, it is the cry of Israel (Exod. 2:23–25) that mobilizes YHWH to the action that begins the history of Israel. The cry initiates history.[25] Paul Hanson has shown that the same right of appeal in the form of lament appears in Israel's legal material (Exod. 22:22–24), in which the poor can cry out.[26] While the cry is addressed to YHWH, it is clear that the cry is not merely a religious gesture but has important and direct links to social processes. When such a cry functions as a legal accusation, the witness of the tradition is that YHWH hears and acts (see Ps. 107:4–32). In the Book of the Covenant, we are given two such legal provisions. In the first case (Exod. 22:22–24), YHWH responds to the cry and "kills with a sword." In the second case (v. 27), YHWH hears and is compassionate. In both cases, the cry mobilizes God in the arena of public life. In neither case is the response simple religious succor; it is juridical action that rescues and judges. That is the nature of the function of lament in Israel.

Where the lament is absent, the normal mode of the theodicy question is forfeited.[27] When the lament form is censured, justice questions cannot be asked and eventually become invisible and illegitimate. Instead, we learn to settle for questions of "meaning,"[28] and we reduce the issues to resolutions of love. But the categories of meaning and love do not touch the public systemic questions about which biblical faith is relentlessly concerned. A community of faith that negates laments soon concludes that the hard issues of justice are improper questions to pose at the throne, because the throne seems to be only a place of praise. I believe it thus follows that if justice questions are improper questions at the throne (which is a conclusion drawn through liturgic use), they soon appear to be improper questions in public places, in schools, in hospitals, with the government, and eventually even in the courts. Justice questions disappear into civility and docility.[29] The order of the day comes to seem absolute, beyond question, and we are left with only grim obedience and eventually despair. The point of access for serious change has been forfeited when the propriety of this speech form is denied.

IV

I have pursued the loss of lament in two directions. On the one hand, I have argued in a psychological direction about object relations and ego development. On the other hand, I have argued in a sociological direction concerning public, social questions of justice. I do not intend that the question of lament should be slotted as, or reduced to, either the psychological or the sociological dimension. Rather, the lament makes an assertion about God: that this dangerous, available God matters in *every* dimension of life. Where God's dangerous availability is lost because we fail to carry on our part of the difficult conversation, where God's vulnerability and passion are removed from our speech, we are consigned to anxiety and despair, and the world as we now have it becomes absolutized.

Our understanding of faith is altered dramatically depending on whether God is a dead cipher who cannot be addressed and is only the silent *guarantor* of the status quo, or whether God can be addressed in risky ways as the *transformer* of what has not yet appeared. With reference to psychological issues, ego development is not dependent solely on a "good-enough" mother[30] but on a God whose omnipotence is reshaped by pathos.[31] With reference to social questions, the emergence of justice depends not simply on social structures but on a sovereign agent outside the system to whom effective appeal can be made against the system. Ego-strength and social justice finally drive us to theological issues.

A God who must always be praised and never assaulted correlates with a development of "False Self" and an uncritical status quo. But a God who is available in assault correlates with the emergence of genuine self and the development of serious justice.

V

Finally, I conclude with some brief comments on Psalm 39, to see how these claims are worked out in a specific text. Psalm 39 is a lament that makes petition to YHWH. The speaker announces a long-standing intention to keep silent (vv. 1–3a). But the practice of restraint had only contributed to the trouble. In verse 3b, finally there is speech, because the submissive silence is inadequate. In verse 4, the speaker names YHWH for the first time. In that moment of speech of bold address, things already begin to change. The cause of trouble has now become an open question in the relationship. The speaker resolves no longer to be "silent in the face of wickedness," and that resolve creates new possibilities. Verses 4–6 are a meditation on the limits and transitoriness of human life. There is an appeal to know the end, that is, the outcome, but it is not a very vigorous statement. It is still reflective, without great self-assertion.

The mood changes abruptly in verse 7, where God is addressed for the second time. The text has *'adonai* ("lord"), but some evidence suggests a second reading of *YHWH*. But the crucial rhetorical move is *we'atta* ("and now").[32] A major turn is marked as the speech moves from meditation to active, insistent hope.

> And now, what do I hope for [*qwh*]?
> My hope [*yhl*] is in you.

The focus on YHWH is an insistence that things need not and will not stay as they are. This is followed in verse 8 by a powerful imperative, *ntsl* ("snatch" or "deliver"). In verse 9, the petition grows bolder because now the speaker is able to say, *"You have done it."* The silence has turned to accusation, but the accusation is a form of active hope. Verse 11 returns to a more reflective tone. Then, in verse 12 (my trans.), the third reference to YHWH is again a vigorous imperative:

> Hear my prayer, YHWH,
> to my cry give ear,
> at my tears do not be silent,
> for I am a sojourner with you.

The speech that has ended the silence is a strong urging to YHWH. As the speaker has refused silence, now the speaker petitions YHWH also to break the silence (v. 12). The speech of the petitioner seeks to evoke the speech and intervention of YHWH.

The psalm ends with the terse *'enenni* ("I will not be"). The urging is that God should act before the speaker ceases to be, as a result of a process of social nullification. Whether the speaker ceases to be depends on YHWH's direct intervention against powerful forces that practice nullification.

I submit that this psalm makes contact with both points I have argued. On the one hand, the speaker moves from silence to speech.[33] The speech consists of a series of bold imperatives, and it states a clarification that may be read as an indictment of God: "You have done it" (v. 9). The psalm evidences courage and ego-strength before YHWH that permits an act of hope, expectant imperatives, and an insistence that things be changed before it is too late.[34] The insistence addressed to YHWH is matched by a sense of urgency about the threat of not-being. I take this threat to be social and worked through the social system.

On the other hand, the justice questions are raised. They are raised as early as verse 1 with reference to the wicked (*rasha'*).[35] We are not given any specifics, but the reference to "guest" in verse 12 suggests that the question concerns social power and social location that have left the speaker exposed, vulnerable, and without security (except with YHWH).[36] YHWH is reminded that YHWH is responsible for such a sojourner and is called to accountability on their behalf because "I am your passing guest [=sojourner]."

On grounds of both ego-assertion and public justice, Psalm 39 causes a change in heaven with a derivative resolution of social systems on earth. This psalm characteristically brings to speech the cry of a troubled earth (v. 12). Where the cry is not voiced, heaven is not moved and history is not initiated. The end is hopelessness. Where the cry is seriously voiced, heaven may answer and earth may have a new chance. The new resolve in heaven and the new possibility on earth depend on the initiation of protest.

VI

It makes one wonder about the price of our civility, that this chance in our faith has largely been lost because the lament psalms have dropped out of the functioning canon. In that loss, we may unwittingly endorse a "False Self" that can take no initiative toward an omnipotent God. We may also unwittingly endorse unjust systems about which no questions can properly be raised. In the absence of lament, we may be engaged in uncritical history-stifling praise. Both *psychological inauthenticity* and *social immobility* may be derived from the loss of these texts. If we care about authenticity and justice, the recovery of these texts is urgent.

Questions for Reflection

1. Where do you see evidence in your community that removing lament as a form of speech and faith reinforces the status quo in which injustice can persist?

2. Reflect on the correlation of mother-child to God-worshiper with object-relations theory in mind. How does a genuine covenantal relationship in which lament is allowed result in the development of a responsible faith where genuine obedience is possible?

3. Where do you see lament as complaint or protest against injustice being silenced today by systems in power? How does that dynamic play out in your church? In your community? What is the result of negating lament in favor of praise, when hard questions about justice are delegitimized as improper?

4. Lament makes the assertion that God is available, addressable, and ultimately the transformer of the world. Use Psalm 39 as a model for your own insistently hopeful lament about a matter of injustice that is weighing on you.

Chapter 10

The Fearful Thirst for Dialogue

*A*ccording to the great Jewish critic George Steiner,

> [i]t is the Hebraic intuition that God is capable of all speech acts
> except that of monologue, which has generated our acts of reply,
> of questioning, and counter-creation. After the Book of Job and
> Euripides' *Bacchae*, there *had* to be, if man was to bear his being,
> the means of dialogue with God, which are spelled out in our poet-
> ics, music, art.[1]

Steiner's point is that great art must be dialogic, and that great
art is possible only if it is rooted in faith in a God who is dialogic,
a holy agent who engages interactively with creaturely subjects in
a mutuality that impinges upon both parties. From that theological
conviction, I extrapolate that the work of the church in its preoccupation with God's holiness is to bear witness to dialogic holiness
and to engage in the practice of that dialogic holiness. My thesis is
that the church is a venue for dialogue in the midst of a monologic
culture that finds such dialogue to be an unbearable threat that must
be mightily resisted. Dialogue, however, is a practice that is congruent with our deepest nature, made as we are in the image of a
dialogic God.

In our society and in our churches, we are sore tempted to monologue. In the public arena, the military-economic hegemony of the
United States exercises a monologic practice of power that by force
imposes its will on others and silences voices to the contrary. The
same propensity is evident in government that is now largely co-opted
and controlled by wealthy interests that amount to nothing less than an

oligarchy wherein voices of need can scarcely be heard. It is not very different in the churches, wherein judgments are made and positions taken that sound with absolute certainty, without any sense either that God's own life in the world is dialogical or that there is inevitable slippage between God's will and our perception of that will.

Such monologic practice seeks to silence, and such imposed silence kills.[2] The hope of US imperialism is to silence voices to the contrary. The manipulation of the media, moreover, is an effort to still the critical voice of a free press. Such silencing in the long run will kill the spirit of our democracy and create an environment of distrust and resentment that will readily issue in violence. In the church as in our society, such silencing does immense damage, robbing the church of its healing capacity and diverting its energy from missional transformation to keeping the lid of control upon the body.

When individuals or groups arrive at absolute certainty and claim to identify their own view with the mind of God, they engage in profound denial about the complexity and conundrums that constitute the self. Such repressed, denied complexity issues at least in alienation and at worst in violence toward neighbor or self. Most of us, in our seasons of denial, do not go so far as overt violence; but every congregation knows about the absolute, one-dimensional selves of shrill certitude that function as profound impediments to the life and faith of the body.

My thesis is that the church—summoned, formed, and empowered by the God of all dialogue—has in our anxiety-driven society an opportunity to be deeply dialogical about the most important issues, dialogical in a way that keeps our judgments penultimate before the holy throne of God. And the evidence of Scripture provides data for such a theological practice. After naming several obvious examples of dialogue, I focus on two texts of dialogue that have preoccupied me.

1. In the remarkable text of Genesis 18:16–33, God has resolved to destroy the city of Sodom, but Abraham confronts God about that decision. Our translations follow the rabbis' adjustment to Genesis 18:22, so that "Abraham remained standing before the LORD." But before that theological adjustment, the text read, "YHWH remained standing before Abraham." That is, in the earlier version, Abraham is the senior partner in the dialogue

and calls YHWH to account, bargaining YHWH down to a min-
yan of ten righteous people in a clear dialogic act of chutzpah.
2. Moses undertakes a similar dialogic challenge to YHWH in
Exodus 32. YHWH is prepared to consume Israel because of
the production of the golden calf, but this harsh act of judgment
is delayed by the dialogic intervention of Moses. The narrative
reports, in response to the plea of Moses (vv. 11–13), "YHWH
changed his mind" (v. 14).
3. And Job engages YHWH in the most extreme exchange in the
Old Testament. As we know, God's whirlwind speech trumps
Job and seems to reduce him to silence. But in the end, YHWH
says of Job, speaking to Job's conventional, predictable friends,
"You have not spoken of me what is right, as has my servant Job"
(Job 42:7–8). The conclusion I draw is that Job's willingness to
engage YHWH and to challenge both conventional theology and
the justice of God is welcomed by the God of daring dialogue.[3]

These three cases are most striking examples of the dialogue of
ancient Israel with God. I take these texts as background, because
unless with Steiner we know that God is dialogical, we will never
understand that truth takes dialogical form among members of
church and society in a way that precludes ready settlement. Such
theological awareness requires among us a huge unlearning of conventional monologic theology in the church and of monologic patterns of authority in society. The manifestation of a dialogical God
becomes the premise for dialogical human community that precludes
both absolute authority and absolute submissiveness. In every case
of dialogue I have cited, the human partner to the exchange exhibits
enormous energy and courage to enter the zone of holy power and
issue self-announcement.

This same chutzpah before the throne is evident in many psalms
of complaint. In the Old Testament the community of faith—and
by inference the human community—has an enormous stake in dialogue that subverts the destructive combination of authoritarianism
and submissiveness. The breaking of silence that makes newness
possible is nicely voiced in Psalm 39:

I said, "I will guard my ways
    that I may not sin with my tongue;

> I will keep a muzzle on my mouth
>> as long as the wicked are in my presence."
> I was silent and still;
>> I held my peace to no avail;
> my distress grew worse,
>> my heart became hot within me.
> While I mused, the fire burned;
>> then I spoke with my tongue.
>
> vv. 1–3

Everything in faith depends on such utterance.

I want now to conduct two forays into the Psalms as practices of dialogue, with the general insistence that the church in dialogue represents a transformative sub-version of society and church in monologue. Such dialogic practice is at the heart of our faith. It requires courage and energy, and it yields newness that can never be generated through monologue.

First, in Psalm 35 the human person is himself/herself an ongoing internal conversation that is conducted before God. My own experience of such conversation is that during the day when I am awake and in control, I can give expression to my life in a single voice. At night, however, when I am defenseless, all the other voices sound, and the honoring of them becomes the condition of my emerging humanness. Thus, my first example is in the direction of pastoral care and takes place amid our understanding of Freud about the healing capacity of voice and speech. Freud's modern theories clearly are deeply rooted in what he knew intuitively of Jewish interpretive practice.[4]

Psalm 35 is a fairly standard lament psalm with the usual accents on complaint that tells God how bad and urgent the need is and petition that recruits God to be active and effective amid the voiced trouble. What interests me is that this psalm, more than any other I know, includes a candid announcement of the complexity of voices that make a single integrated person a continuing work in progress. I identify four voices that constitute something of a sociogram of the life and practice of faith.

In verses 1–3, the psalm begins with a series of six imperative petitions that are addressed to YHWH. The first five are "contend," "fight," "take hold," "rise up," and "draw." The imagery mixes the judicial and the military, asking God to be both judge and warrior.

But the sixth imperative is the one that interests us: "Say to my soul, 'I am your salvation.'" After the vigorous and violent petitions, this sixth imperative asks YHWH to speak, to break the silence. The ultimate yearning of this petition is that God should speak, enter into dialogue, and offer assurance. The speaker daringly proposes to YHWH what is to be said and who is to be addressed: "Address me, my soul, my *nephesh*, my life."

As with many psalms, this rhetoric is so familiar and conventional that we do not notice. This simple voice of petition is speaking truth to power and is requiring from YHWH a quite specific answer. The proposed answer cuts through the neglect, silence, and absence of God, and offers assurance that God is back in play—in my life—with enough power and sufficient attentiveness to change everything. The suggested response echoes the old liturgic traditions that scholars call salvation oracles, which are best known from the exile-ending proclamation of Second Isaiah (see Isa. 41:8–10, 13; 43:1–3, 5).

Israel—like this psalmist—does not doubt that God's self-announcement will change everything; but the self-announcement from YHWH does not come from divine initiative, as our usual Augustinian presuppositions might suggest. Rather, what makes newness possible is human utterance of insistence that expects, evokes, and listens for divine announcement of salvation. Even the expected deployment of YHWH depends upon a dialogic initiative by the psalmist.

The psalm proceeds in verses 4–8 with a wish list of imprecations, of bad things proposed to God that God should do to "my enemies." Whatever else we may think about these wishes, we should notice that the speaker is instructing God on the best way to proceed.

After the imperatives, verse 9 turns to a human promise. "Then," only when God has acted decisively at the point of need, the psalmist promises:

> Then my soul [*nephesh*] shall rejoice in the LORD,
> exulting in his deliverance.

The "soul" that rejoices is the same "soul" to whom God was to have said, in verse 3, "I am your salvation." The same self that has listened for God's assurance will now speak. That self, "all my bones"—every part of the self that has been addressed by God—will answer back:

> All my bones shall say,
>   "O Lord, *who is like you?*
> You deliver the weak
>   from those too strong for them,
>   the weak and needy from those who despoil them."
>   v. 10, emphasis added

YHWH is the subject of a "formula of incomparability." Who is like YHWH? No one! No one is like YHWH in power. No one is like YHWH in compassionate attentiveness. YHWH is committed to the weak and the needy; it is this voice of need and weakness that speaks, now a second voice in the conversation. That voice of need has become a voice of gratitude.

After this doxological utterance in verses 9–10, the psalm moves in conventional fashion. In verses 11–14, the speaker is permitted to practice self-absorption as the poem is dominated by first-person pronouns that state need but also evidence of righteousness by having cared for the neighborhood. It is the speaker who, when others were sick, engaged in rites and rituals of grief and healing.

The rhetoric then turns with a disjunctive "but" from self-preoccupation to "they," the same "they" who are the subject of imprecations in verses 4–8:

> But at my stumbling *they* gathered in glee,
>   *they* gathered together against me;
> ruffians whom I did not know
>   tore at me without ceasing;
> *they* impiously mocked more and more,
>   gnashing at me with their teeth.
>   vv. 15–16, emphasis added

They gathered. They tore at me. They mocked more and more. They gnashed their teeth. The poem does not say how this happened; all we know is that they—who remain unnamed—engaged in hostile, antineighborly conduct. Thus, in verses 11–14 the poem is about "me"; in verses 15–16 it is about "they." There is a standoff in this urgent struggle.

But then it becomes clear that this "I–they" presentation is a rhetorical strategy for what comes next. Again, YHWH is named and addressed with a large imperative: "Rescue my *nephesh*!" (v. 17). After this third use of the word *nephesh*, the speaking self, who now depends completely upon YHWH and is without other resources, makes a promise to YHWH that immediately upon the rescue for which he has prayed, there will be ample thanks expressed to YHWH:

> *Then* I will thank you in the great congregation;
> in the mighty throng I will praise you.
> v. 18, emphasis added

The psalmist is apparently not yet convinced that YHWH "gets it," that YHWH understands the critical urgency of the moment. Now with YHWH at attention, the speaker returns to the enemy that threatens. The enemy is now quoted. They speak, as of course they do. In this life-or-death conversation, all parties have opportunity to give utterance. They do not speak *shalom*. Rather, in shamelessness they mock "more and more" (see v. 16):

> For *they* do not speak peace,
> but *they* conceive deceitful words
> against those who are quiet in the land.
> *They* open wide their mouths against me;
> *they* say, "Aha, Aha,
> our eyes have seen it."
> vv. 20–21, emphasis added

That is what they say in their dismissive scorn. The double use of "aha" is a mock that trivializes and embarrasses the psalmist. The speaker in need now is utterly exposed and shamed. The enemies have now seen him in ways in which he did not want to be seen. They have seen him as helpless. And we may imagine, they have also seen that he is resourceless and without an advocate. They are free to bully him because he has no means to protect himself or to injure them. The dismissive utterance of the adversaries not only mocks the speaker; we infer that the enemies also mock the God of the speaker, who has not come to help (see Prov. 17:5). In a shame-oriented society, such voices of derision speak loudly and dangerously.

When the enemy takes part in the conversation in this way, the speaker is again driven to YHWH, who is again named in Ps. 35:22. Then follows a series of urgent petitions, imperatives addressed to the Holy One:

> You have seen, O LORD; do not be silent!
>   O Lord, do not be far from me!
> Wake up! Bestir yourself for *my* defense,
>   for *my* cause, *my* God and *my* Lord!
> Vindicate me, O LORD, *my* God,
>   according to your righteousness,
>   and do not let them rejoice over me.
>   vv. 22–24, emphasis added

The address is to God, but the verses are dominated by first-person references: "My defense, my cause, my God, my Lord." Everything for the speaker is at stake in this summons issued to YHWH. Only YHWH stands as a protector against another dismissive utterance that would, if spoken, be the unbearable extremity of social humiliation:

> Do not let them say in their hearts . . .
> Do not let them say . . .

Stop this voice sounding in my life. It is a loud, threatening voice, and I cannot bear it. We can imagine the speaker turning to God while covering his ears to resist this social dismantling that is at the brink of utterance. What he fears is that the enemy will say:

> Aha,[5] we have our heart's desire.
>   v. 25a

This NRSV translation is an expansion of only two Hebrew words, "Aha, our *nephesh*." Our soul! Our self! The psalmist dreads that his enemies will voice their own satisfied self-affirmation that will signify their triumph and his undoing. The psalmist is afraid that they will gloat:

> Do not let them say, "We have swallowed you up."
>   v. 25b

The prayer continues with more imperatives and petitions. But the speaker, having said everything that could be said about the adversary, now trusts a coming well-being. He knows that he will be "vindicated," that is, treated righteously. He knows this because (in the process of the psalm) he has heard the assurance of YHWH for which he prayed in verse 3. He knows because he has given full voice to the adversary and finds the adversary, through such out-loud utterance, less overwhelming than he had imagined. Thus the speaker can now enjoy a sense of well-being and can imagine himself fully and gladly resituated in his congregation. It is that congregation that will join in praise to the God who saves. The congregation will issue a standard doxology:

> Let those who desire my vindication
> shout for joy and be glad,
> and say evermore,
> "Great is the LORD,
> who delights in the welfare of his servant."
>
> v. 27

This stereotypical phrasing merits close attention, because through it the worshiping congregation connects complex strands of reality. YHWH is praised as "great," but the reason greatness is acknowledged is that the congregation knows that YHWH has taken delight in the *shalom* of this particular speaker. The final voice is the speaker's resolve to put his own tongue to glad work (v. 28). The speaker's tongue will be employed—we may imagine "without ceasing"—to celebrate YHWH's righteousness, YHWH's capacity to take initiative to turn the world of the speaker back to life; the last word is praise all day every day. The very process of the psalm itself permits the speaker to move from *urgent need* to *glad doxology*; we who have paid attention are permitted the same glad move in our lives.

Finally, how does that transformation from need to gladness occur? My answer is that the psalmist has constructed and given voice to a complex conversation that was inchoately present in his life, as it is inescapably present in every life. I imagine, given my own compulsive ruminations at night, that the speaker has heard, imagined, and uttered all four parts of this conversation; he has done so because these voices are characteristically present to us when our faith becomes honest:

- There is the voice of *the saving God* who will—soon or late—say to the needy one,

  > "I am your salvation."
  > v. 3

- There is the voice of *the speaker* who anticipates that in time to come—soon, but not very soon—he will be able to make glad affirmation:

  > All my bones shall say,
  >   "O LORD, who is like you?
  > You deliver the weak
  >   from those too strong for them,
  >   the weak and needy from those who despoil them."
  > v. 10

- There is the voice of *the adversary* that rings in our ears. Indeed, the adversary gets the most airtime for mockery:

  > "Aha, Aha.
  > Our eyes have seen it."
  > v. 21

  In addition to what they have said, this is what they might say that I cannot bear to hear:

  > "Aha, we have our heart's desire. . . .
  > We have swallowed you up."
  > v. 25

- This dread-filled exchange, however, does not happen in a vacuum. The psalmist remembers that he is a member of *the community*. And as he can anticipate—with dread—what the adversary might say, so he can anticipate—with elation—what the congregation will say in time to come:

  > "Great is the LORD,
  > who delights in the welfare of his servant."
  > v. 27b

During the day, the speaker might imagine his entire life in the single, unified, coherent, manageable self-announcement. But at night, that singular coherence falls apart into a cacophony of voices, all of which press for airtime. The speaker finds now that his life is reconstituted as a dialogic transaction in which everything is at stake:

> Here speaks *threat* that will undo;
> Here speaks *holy intervention* that will rescue;
> Here speaks *self in confidence*;
> Here speaks *congregation* in a summation of
> God's goodness toward the speaker.

This poem is a remarkable artistic achievement. It is of course only a poem. But it is a poem that bespeaks the contested dialogue that constitutes life in faith under stress.

1. We can imagine that this is a *liturgical articulation* in which all voices are routinely acknowledged as commonplace in faith, for this dialogic faith knows about the contest between YHWH and the adversary who vie for control of our lives.

2. But we can also imagine that behind the commonplace liturgical expression is the deep pathos of *profound personal struggle* by one haunted with all of these voices. Newness, as we know, can come only when these inchoate voices are given freedom of tongue. It may be that in such a rhetorical map of turmoil, dispute, and anxiety, the speaker must play all of the parts, because these voices are all parts of the self.[6] But even if the speaker speaks each role, each voice is given different nuance and inflection, because these are identifiable voices in a divided, conflicted self. Every self that pays attention to the rich internal life entrusted to us by God knows about being haunted, knows about the voices of threat, knows about the care of the congregation, knows about the holy possibility of God, and knows about the work that the self must conduct. The happy reality is that in ancient Israel, public and pastoral venues were available to give these voices airtime.

3. Liturgical commonplace and pathos-filled struggle of candor mark this psalm. Read in a psychological direction, we can see that this is not an exceptionally disordered life, for every attentive life is a conversation that is on its way to articulation. But I do not reduce

the psalm to psychology. Let us imagine that the psalm is a *mapping out of social forces*, a field of complex power that is real in the perception of faith:

> There really is a *yearning, needy self*;
> there really are voices of *dismantling threat*,
>   anciently remembered and contemporarily uttered;
> there really is a *surrounding congregation*
>   that has not lost its confidence, buoyancy, or nerve;
> and to be sure, there really is a *holy God* who waits offstage
>   to be summoned to intervene decisively.

This is the world where God has placed us, and the self is characteristically at risk among these voices. This self at risk makes its tricky way amid all these voices in a move from need to praise. The voices are real and they are parts of the self. The voices sound in nighttime moments of vulnerability. Freud, of course, already understood that to give concrete utterance to such voices is to rob the negating voices of authority. Conversely, to give utterance is to let healthy reality override the threat.

This psalm, unlike many others, is an affirmation that life is deeply contested, a dialogue in which everything is at stake. Where we fail such pastoral, liturgical articulation, we are fated, I suggest, to a monologic world of repression and denial that can host no newness and has immense and recurring destructive force. The action of such recital is to see that one's life is an open venue for God's unsettled, unresolved contestation; all parts of the self, all social realities, all forces converge in the utterance that permits newness. The challenge for the teaching pastors of the church is to authorize and enact the conversation that breaks the monologic grip of dominant ideology, whether that ideology be of the military-industrial complex or of our well-meaning parents. To break the grip is to forswear control and domination, and to enter a practice of vulnerability that is our true human habitat.

I note one other remarkable rhetorical maneuver that occurs three times in this psalm:

- In 35:9 the psalmist pledges to rejoice in the Lord, once God carries out the actions against his enemies that he commends in verses 4–8.

- In verse 17, the psalmist petitions God in an imperative to "rescue me from their ravages," and then promises to give thanks in verse 18.
- In verse 27, the psalmist urges God to let the congregation celebrate his deliverance, and then commits in verse 28 to testify to God's righteousness "all day long."

In each case the psalmist promises to praise and give God thanks on the condition that God acts to deliver.[7] Indeed, praise of God is consequent to and dependent upon God's action of rescue.

I cite this rhetorical maneuver because it indicates that the psalmist, as the lesser party to the dialogue, has nerve and entitlement to hold his ground in a Job-like fashion and to make demands on the senior party to the dialogue. This means that the dialogue is not cheap or easy or facile; rather it consists in a struggle for mutual validation, with the outcome held in abeyance for the future. But that, of course, is the character of dialogue that refuses premature conclusion or closure. Dialogic partners wait together, even if not comfortably, for newness to emerge in the process between them, a newness that might to some extent satisfy both parties. In this case, that expected emergent satisfaction will be *rescue* for the psalmist and *praise* for God.

The second facet of dialogic life in a monologic environment I will deal with more briefly. It is the capacity of the Psalms—Israel's script for worship and faithful imagination—to move from the most intent concrete personal experience to the great public agenda of the congregation. The interface of personal and public puts the one and the many into a conversation of mutuality. I suggest that this characteristic maneuver in the congregation is an important antidote to both the privatization of much of the life of the church and the loud moral indignation of the church without the specificities of pathos and hope.

We have seen this motif at work in Psalm 35 in two references. In verse 18, after the anticipated rescue by God, the psalmist says:

> Then I will thank you in the great congregation;
>   in the mighty throng I will praise you.

The thanks is an individual matter in which the speaker runs the course of need and the concreteness of divine intervention.[8] But that specific thanks is in "the great congregation," so that we may imagine members of the community gathered around, giving praise for miracles that are never evoked, never acknowledged, never celebrated, and never publicly owned in a world of monologic control. The same motif, less directly expressed, is also evident in verse 27:

> Let those who desire my vindication
> shout for joy and be glad,
> and say evermore,
> "Great is the LORD,
> who delights in the welfare of his servant."

The congregation consists in those who "desire my vindication," who are pleased at God's righteous action on my behalf. The speaker can imagine, even in great need, that the congregation is filled with members who care, who are praying for and pulling for, and who are cheering God with reference to a concrete rescue.

Even the most personal of prayers in the Psalter are in the horizon of the congregation. Indeed, Fredrik Lindström has vigorously argued that the Psalter is all about temple theology, about a place of centered divine presence, power, and attentiveness.[9] This communal sense of the individual is of immense importance in a society that is increasingly organized to resist any notion of the public and to isolate individuals so as to leave us all disconnected and at the mercy of market forces. Efforts to dismantle Social Security may be taken as a microcosm for the efforts of a monologic society to preclude the true human functioning of the social. When we become aware that genuine security is inescapably social, the privatization of society, taken theologically, is a decision to be insecure. This dialogic alternative to monologue is a call to be "members one of another."

I will cite two clear cases of the move from personal to public whereby the claim of personal miracle evokes public thanks and praise, whereby individual thanksgiving funds the imagination and energy of the entire public.

Psalm 30 is a pure song of individual thanksgiving. At the center of the psalm, the speaker narrates the dramatic experience:

- initial well-being (vv. 6–7ab);
- devastating disruption (v. 7cd);

- petition and bargaining with God (vv. 8–10); and
- resolution and well-being (v. 11).

That drama is intensely personal. It culminates, moreover, in the resolve of the recipient of God's mercy to praise and give thanks forever:

> So that my soul may praise you and not be silent.
> O LORD my God, I will give thanks to you forever.
>
> v. 12

The speaker is totally focused on the journey of the self at the behest of God.

The psalm begins in a quite intimate, personal testimony:

> I will extol you, O LORD, for you have drawn me up,
>   and did not let my foes rejoice over me.
> O LORD my God, I cried to you for help,
>   and you have healed me.
> O LORD, you brought up my soul from Sheol,
>   restored me to life from among those gone down to the Pit.
>
> vv. 1–3

But then the psalmist moves beyond self. He knows that the joy and elation at his new life is too much for him to celebrate alone. He appeals to his community and recruits others to join in the celebration:

> Sing praises to the LORD, O you his faithful ones,
>   and give thanks to his holy name.
>
> v. 4

The summons is to "his faithful ones," the ones who are steadfast and keep covenant. They are the ones who are schooled in the dialogic practice of fidelity, for they will understand the dramatic turn in his life. They not only will fully appreciate that turn, but they will know whom to credit with it and how best to acknowledge it. Indeed, it is the work of the faithful congregation to take up individual cases and magnify and enhance them by full public coverage. The community knows that divine love outdistances divine neglect or anger. They know about the hardness and sadness of the night that seems interminable when the haunting voice of death stalks our beds. They are the ones who have learned, amid these voices of the night, that the powerful threats of the night must flee and yield when God gives the sun:

> For his anger is but for a moment;
>   his favor is for a lifetime.
> Weeping may linger for the night,
>   but joy comes with the morning.
>
> v. 5

The congregation consists in those who have been there before us and before this speaker. They know of case after case of suffering turned to well-being and death turned to life, anger to grace, and weeping to joy.

Indeed Israel's self-understanding is rooted in that characteristic transformative act. The overarching awareness in ancient Israel is, of course, the exile, that harsh moment of displacement. In that context, the poetry of Second Isaiah sounds, on God's lips, a recognition very like Psalm 30:5:

> For a brief moment I abandoned you,
>   but with great compassion I will gather you.
> In overflowing wrath for a moment
>   I hid my face from you,
> but with everlasting love I will have compassion on you,
>   says the LORD, your Redeemer.
>
> Isa. 54:7–8

The congregation knows, as God here concedes, that there really are moments of divine abandonment when we must honestly say, "My God, my God, why have you forsaken me?" They know about the hidden face of absence. But they are also able to trust and anticipate that as the sun rises, so the great compassion and everlasting love of the redeemer God are beyond such abandonment.

If we ask, how does the congregation so confidently know this, the answer is, by many individual testimonies to which this one in Psalm 30 is now added. The truth of miracle is not from above in some theoretical imposition. Rather, the truth of miracle is from below, from wonders that are daily, concrete, material, and specific. And the congregation joins in doxology because no one can celebrate the miracle alone. This security is indeed social without at all minimizing the first-person-singular articulation.

The same dynamic practice occurs in the more familiar Psalm 22. The first familiar part of the psalm is quite intimate and personal, and struggles with the reality of divine abandonment (vv. 1–21a). The psalm turns in the middle of verse 21 with the abrupt, inexplicable affirmation:

> From the horns of the wild oxen you have answered me.

That simple utterance affirms that the prayer of petition in the foregoing verses has been effective. The petition has moved God to overcome abandonment and to answer, that is, to be dialogically present in a context of profound need.

But then the speaker, now rescued, affirmed, and addressed, must find a way to give voice to newness that is commensurate with a need that has been previously expressed. Immediately the speaker knows that he cannot do this task of acknowledgment by himself, but must recruit his companions into the task. He knows how to proceed:

> I will tell of your name to my brothers and sisters;
> in the midst of the congregation I will praise you.
> v. 22

It is a telling, a narrating, a bearing witness. The first hearers are "brothers," that is, fellow members of the covenant who inhabit the congregation. No privatism here! Verse 22 is followed by a much larger invitation to share the joy:

> You who fear the LORD, praise him!
> All you offspring of Jacob, glorify him;
> stand in awe of him, all you offspring of Israel!
> v. 23

All celebrate the truth that God hears, answers, and thereby transforms. As Ellen Davis has shown, the Bible characteristically moves in concentric circles from particular embodied truth to the larger communal acclamation as all are drawn into the utterance of joy.[10]

Verse 25 expands the reference to the congregation to "the great congregation," the same phrase we saw in 35:18:

> From you comes my praise in the great congregation.
>   22:25a

In the move from "congregation" to "great congregation," the circle expands even more. After that, it is "all the ends of the earth" and "all the families of the nations," all of whom celebrate the rule of YHWH over all nations:

> All the ends of the earth shall remember
>   and turn to the LORD;
> and all the families of the nations
>   shall worship before him.
> For dominion belongs to the LORD,
>   and he rules over the nations.
>   vv. 27–28

In 22:28, the psalm clearly employs rhetoric that moves out from the personal to the great public affirmation about the rule of God over the nation-states. The psalm accomplishes this transition easily and readily, for both the personal and the public have to do with overcoming alienation for the sake of *shalom.*

In a final leap of inclusiveness, the psalm now refers to praise among the deceased who are now only remembered, along with the ones only hoped for and not yet born:

> To him, indeed, shall all who sleep in the earth bow down;
>   before him shall bow all who go down to the dust,
>   and I shall live for him.
> Posterity will serve him;
>   future generations will be told about the Lord,
> and proclaim his deliverance to a people yet unborn,
>   saying that he has done it.
>   vv. 29–31

The whole of creation is gathered around this one speaker. That speaker initiated the process by telling the truth of divine abandonment. The deep reality of divine abandonment, however, did not lead to silence and resignation. Rather, it led to vigorous protest, accusation, and petition that eventuated in divine attentiveness. And if we wonder why abandonment led to speech, it is because everything in this dialogic community leads to speech. Israel knows, and after Israel, Sigmund Freud and Martin Luther King and many others, that utterance produces newness. Utterance enlivens social possibility, but it enlivens social possibility because we—all of us—are in the image of the dialogic God. Praise, the alternative voice of this community, is not easy speech; it arises only after the hard trouble is told, truth that is hard on all powerful ears, including the ears of the powerful God.

So imagine church leaders presiding over and empowering communities of utterance who tell truth that leads to newness. We have the script and we have the venue. It is a ministry of Word, and it is a ministry of sacrament, because the sacrament enacts bodily what our words dare say. And every time a leader empowers a community of utterance, we commit a subversive act that intends to overthrow the powers of silence.

I do not know our way ahead in North American society. But I do know that we live in a silencing culture, growing more silent amid electronic prattle. The empire depends on quiescent taxpayers. The market depends on isolated shoppers. As we grow quiescent and isolated, the human spirit withers, and options for newness grow jaded in fatigue. And then this utterance of truth and possibility, dangerous and welcome, so dangerous as to be not very welcome, but nonetheless urgent.

I finish with the narrative of Bartimaeus. When Bartimaeus heard that it was Jesus of Nazareth, he shouted out, "Jesus, Son of David, have mercy on me." Mark reports:

Many sternly ordered him to be quiet, but he cried out even more loudly, "Son of David, have mercy on me!" (10:48)

And the rest, as we say, is history. The world is filled with librarian-like people who infuse silence into our common life. But the cry breaks that open:

Weeping may linger for the night,
   but joy comes with the morning.
                  Ps. 30:5b

All these words have been entrusted to us by the Word become flesh, full of grace and dialogic truth.

Questions for Reflection

1. What elements of our Christian worship exhibit attention to the practice of dialogic holiness? Where do you see the need for more vulnerable dialogue in our liturgies and affirmations of our faith?

2. What monologic patterns of authority and theology do you need to unlearn? How can the Psalms play a role in that unlearning for you personally, and as part of a worshiping community? How can pastors and worship leaders "authorize and enact" the sort of honest conversations demonstrated in the Psalms?

3. Brueggemann uses Psalm 35 to identify four voices of faith under stress: *the saving God, the speaker, the adversary, and the community.* What voices can you name that contribute to your internal conversations in the metaphorical middle of the night? Which voices dominate?

4. The Psalms provide a script for worship that allows for the expansion of concentric circles of truth and praise, making space for private personal experience to be shared in the midst of the public agenda of a community. How does your community of faith demonstrate the attentive care of the whole toward the needs of the individual? What opportunities for collective praise in response to individual testimony are available?

PART FOUR

Hope and Thanksgiving

Chapter 11

The Wonder of Thanks, Specific and Material

*I*n the book of Psalms *praise* and *thanks* tend to converge and are treated as synonyms (as in Ps. 30:4), but they are in fact very different. Whereas praise tends to be expansive and nonspecific, thanks is typically focused on a particular memorable gift from God that evokes gratitude. Gratitude is thus concrete and expressed in both *verbal form* (as a song of thanksgiving) and *material form* (as a thank-offering). Israel's usual way of giving thanks is by telling: reciting a narrative about a situation of need or desperation and then reporting on the wondrous way in which God rescued, delivered, or restored.

Psalm 30

As seen in chapter 10, Psalm 30 is a clear and concise narrative account of thanks. At the outset the speaker remembers being prosperous and self-assured:

> As for me, I said in my prosperity,
> "I shall never be moved."
> By your favor, O Lord,
>   you had established me as a strong mountain.
>   vv. 6–7a

That good life, however, is abruptly disturbed. And God is the cause:

> you hid your face;
>   I was dismayed.
>   v. 7b

The move from *prosperity* to *dismay* is quick and complete. We are not told the particulars of the case, but clearly the speaker has a specific event in mind. The speaker can remember, then, that he prayed ("cried") to YHWH in his desperation. This speaker quotes his own earlier complaint, uttered at that time. His complaint includes rhetorical questions that seek to motivate YHWH to act (not unlike Ps. 88:10–12) and an urgent petition that God listen, be gracious, and help:

> To you, O LORD, I cried,
>   and to the LORD I made supplication:
> "What profit is there in my death,
>   if I go down to the Pit?
> Will the dust praise you?
>   Will it tell of your faithfulness?
> Hear, O LORD, and be gracious to me!
>   O LORD, be my helper!"
>
> 30:8–10

Everything to this point is remembered action from the past. Then there is a pause in the rhetoric—a pause that regularly occurs when complaint turns to praise. When the psalmist speaks again, all is resolved by God, though we do not know how:

> You have turned my mourning into dancing;
>   you have taken off my sackcloth
>   and clothed me with joy.
>
> v. 11

The culmination of the entire account is gratitude, a response to the resolution in thanks and praise:

> so that my soul may *praise* you and not be silent.
>   O LORD my God, I will give *thanks* to you forever.
>
> v. 12

In short compass, the speaker has taken us through the entire drama of *prosperity*, *dismay*, *complaint*, and *resolution*. The speaker refers to a specific deliverance. But that specificity is not identified. As a result, when we belatedly use Psalm 30, we may bring to it our own specificity of *prosperity*, *dismay*, *complaint*, and *resolution*.

The verdict the psalmist reaches is that God's anger is short term and God's favor is very long term:

> For his anger is but for a moment;
> his favor is for a lifetime.
> Weeping may linger for the night,
> but joy comes with the morning.
>
> v. 5

It is no wonder that there will be "thanks to you forever" (v. 12). The new life of the speaker is grounded in gratitude. God has done for him what he could not do for himself! The hope, when we belatedly use Psalm 30, is that the psalmist's verdict will be our own as well.

Psalm 107

A fuller rendition of the same practice of thanks is voiced in Psalm 107. The poem begins with a summons to give thanks. The speaker assumes that the "redeemed" and the "gathered" share his gratitude to God and will want to join in expression of it (vv. 1–3). The body of the psalm consists of four case studies in rescue that invite and evoke gratitude:

- those lost in the desert (vv. 4–9);
- those in prison (vv. 10–16);
- those sick (vv. 17–22);
- those at sea in a storm (vv. 23–32).

The pattern of the narrative is highly stylized. In each case, the context of trouble is described in hyperbolic language. The purpose of this kind of rhetoric is to make clear that the subjects expressing this trouble were completely helpless on their own. In each case, however, the extreme circumstances did not lead to despair. They led, rather, to prayers of petition addressed to YHWH as "cry." The "cry" is not elaborated on, but it clearly consisted of a complaint and a petition whereby God was moved to act. And in each case, we are told, God delivered! That divine response, according to the psalmist's rhetoric, is immediate and complete. Without delay, God acted decisively to extricate the petitioners from desperate circumstance.

In each case, the deliverance wrought by YHWH evoked thanks. This thanks was in response to God's covenantal reliability (steadfast love) that had been exhibited. In each instance, it is affirmed to Israel that God is reliable, responsive, and capable of restorative transformation. The theological claims made here for YHWH are very broad, but the evidence is specific and remarkable:

- rescue from desert abandonment;
- emancipation from prison, even if there for rebelling;
- healing of immobilizing illness;
- stilling of a storm.

In three of the four cases, there is an invitation to thank God for the prompt and effective rescue (vv. 8, 15, 31). In the third case, however, there is an important variation in the rhetoric of gratitude:

Let them thank the LORD for his steadfast love,
    for his wonderful works to humankind.
And let them offer thanksgiving sacrifices,
    and tell of his deeds in songs of joy.
                                    vv. 21–22

In this instance, the appropriate response to a divine miracle, beyond verbalizing or singing one's thanks, is a *sacrifice of thanks*. The grateful person is called on to give an expression of gratitude by animal sacrifice. Along with the verbal rendition of the "wonders" wrought by God, gratitude is to be given a concrete, material expression by offering of something valuable, a "thank-offering." This particular kind of offering is specified in the inventory of sacrifices in Leviticus 7:15–18, where it is distinguished as a "freewill offering," that is, a spontaneous act beyond regulation, in response to inexplicable generosity on God's part. In the familiar text of Micah 6:6–8, moreover, there is a probing of what may constitute an appropriate thanksgiving offering, which is to say, "what is asked for." The prophet wonders what may be an adequate material object to give to God: perhaps calves, rams, olive oil in large quantities, even the firstborn son. Something of value clearly. The conclusion, however, in perfect line with prophetic emphases, is that the proper offering is covenantal responsiveness expressed as neighbor love. *That* is the real thank-offering:

> He has told you, O mortal, what is good;
> and what does the LORD require of you
> but to do justice, and to love kindness,
> and to walk humbly with your God?
>
> 6:8

Micah moves past *material offerings* to *relational realities* that are even more demanding. But the point is the same: Gratitude entails serious, responsive engagement that disrupts "business as usual."

In the Psalms, the "reason" for thanks is invariably a "wonderful work," that is, a miracle from YHWH that defies human explanation and that is beyond human capacity.[1] The sequence of thanks is thus as follows: *dire need > petition > rescue > thanks*, all of which must be narrated. This is the characteristic sequence by which Israel specifies—often in great detail—why it is so grateful. There is nothing "matter of fact" about these wondrous experiences that evoke gratitude. What evokes gratitude is an act *outside* all normal categories of cause and effect. Because that decisive turn of circumstance defies all reasonableness, gratitude too, in similar manner, is beyond reasonableness. There is no quid pro quo in gratitude. It is evoked by wonder and expressed in generosity to the point of extravagance. Israel cannot thank YHWH enough! Or do enough in thanks for what YHWH has done!

After the four case studies, the remainder of the psalm ruminates on God's unimaginable, wondrous power:

- *He turns* rivers into deserts . . . a fruitful land into salty waste; (Ps. 107:33–34, my trans.)
- *He turns* deserts into water . . . hunger into liveliness; (vv. 35–36, my trans.)
- *He pours* contempt . . . ; (v. 40)
- *He raises up* the meek. (v. 41, my trans.)

These articulations of thanks focus on the powerful verbs in which YHWH is agent and subject. These acknowledgments leave us amazed, because we have no conventional categories for such "turns."

This outrageously simple speech thanking God for "miracles" violates our rationality; we do not want to think about an "interventionist" God who acts directly and decisively, if only because such a claim violates our sense of a scientifically reasonable and "explainable" world. This kind of psalmic rhetoric that defies "reason" is at best an embarrassment. It is an embarrassment whenever something happens in our experience that pushes us beyond our explanatory control. When explanatory categories are seen to be inadequate, Israel bursts out in gratitude, no longer embarrassed, with rhetoric that matches and is appropriate to the "wonder" that has been given.

The final declaration of Psalm 107 once again witnesses to God's steadfast love and invites "the wise" to ponder it (v. 43). "The wise" are those who know that more is going on in our lives than can be contained within our explanatory categories. It is the foolish, wise in their own eyes and by their own eyes and by their own lights, who think everything can be "explained." But, as it happens, such explanatory "wisdom" is ultimately foolish, making the rhetoric of gratitude indispensable for the truth of our lives. We read to observe carefully that a life lived in safe, explanatory categories can never arrive at gratitude, because in the safe, explained world there is never anything new beyond our control about which to wonder or to acknowledge.

Psalm 116

Psalm 116 provides an example of the performance of thanks. The speaker acknowledges that God has answered prayer and worked a miracle in his life:

> Because he inclined his ear to me,
>> therefore I will call on him as long as I live.
> The snares of death encompassed me;
>> the pangs of Sheol laid hold on me;
>> I suffered distress and anguish.

Then I called on the name of the LORD;
"O LORD, I pray, save my life!"
vv. 2–4

Like Psalm 30, these lines narrate the entire drama of the "reason for thanks," a reason confided in verse 8:

For you have delivered my soul from death,
    my eyes from tears,
    my feet from stumbling.

Then the speaker asks a question not unlike that of Micah 6:6:

What shall I return to the LORD,
    for all his bounty to me?
Ps. 116:12

The answer is given promptly with direct first-person resolve:

I will lift up the cup of salvation
    and call on the name of the LORD,
I will pay my vows to the LORD
    in the presence of all his people. . . .
I will offer to you a thanksgiving sacrifice
    and call on the name of the LORD.
I will pay my vows to the LORD
    in the presence of all his people,
in the courts of the house of the LORD,
    in your midst, O Jerusalem.
vv. 13–14, 17–19

The four first-person verbs stand out:

- I will lift up.
- I will pay.
- I will offer.
- I will pay.

Thanks and Eucharist

In the Christian tradition, it is possible to trace a route from Israel's practice of thanksgiving to the practice of the Eucharist, which means "thanks." The Gospel of Mark presents two miraculous feedings by Jesus that can be understood as the narrative foundations of the church's practice of Eucharist. In Mark 6:41, where Jesus fed five thousand and had twelve baskets of bread left over, it is said that he "blessed and broke" the bread. In the second narrative, where he fed four thousand and had seven baskets of bread left over, it is said that Jesus gave thanks and broke the bread (8:6). In the second telling, the verb is *eucharistēsas*. Jesus' act is one of thanks to God for bread. The drama of the sacrament in the church, simply and without further liturgical enhancement, is an act of thanks. It is a stylized, material acknowledgment of the wonder of life that is the gift of God. In the Christian tradition, that gift is given in a cruciform narrative, as bread *broken* and wine *poured out*.

The alternative to the drama of gratitude is a sense of self-sufficiency that corresponds, in our society, to free-market ideology in which there is no gratitude, because everything is an act of self-accomplishment. Instead of giving thanks, one is tempted toward and nurtured in accomplishment, achievement, and possession. It is a world in which no gifts are given, no wonders are enacted, and no transformations are noticed. It is a world where one is alone with one's resources and capacities. But this is to act the fool, a dread mistaking of the true nature of reality. We have already seen in Psalm 107:43 that the wise ponder God's generous fidelity. Foolishness, by contrast, notices no such fidelity. The fool in the parable of Luke 12, for example, is perfectly cast as one without gratitude. He can only congratulate himself on his possessions, with no one else to thank:

> And I will say to my soul, Soul, you have ample goods stored up for many years; relax, eat, drink, be merry. (v. 19)

But after he calls himself "soul," he is called by another name that surely surprises him—"fool":

> You fool! This very night your life is being demanded of you. And the things you have prepared, whose will they be? (v. 20)

The fool with no gratitude is the perfect contrast to the wise one who notices God's generosity. In the end, the fool in the parable is condemned as "not rich toward God" (v. 21). Our world, with no gratitude, only self-accomplishments, is shown to be similarly foolish. In sum, gratitude is a sense of being "rich toward God" in response to God's richness toward us. And as it happens, the Eucharist, the church's exposition of Israel's thank-offering, is an act of defiance and resistance against the self-sufficiency championed by the consumer culture in our society. Thanks is a recognition that we live by divine generosity, to which we can, as we are able, render and enact commensurate gratitude. This continuing transaction between *divine generosity* and *human gratitude* is exposited by Paul in his bid for a church offering in 2 Corinthians 8. The act of divine generosity is stated eloquently:

> For you know the generous act of our Lord Jesus Christ, that . . . he became poor, so that by his poverty you might become rich. (v. 9)

On that basis, Paul appeals for the church he addresses to respond generously:

> Now as you excel in everything, . . . so we want you to excel also in this generous undertaking. (v. 7)

The appeal ends in verse 15 with an allusion to the ancient manna narrative, thus tracing God's generosity from *ancient bread* to *eucharistic bread*. According to Paul's account, the close link between divine generosity and human gratitude is defining for the church. For that reason it is no wonder that we sing:

> Now thank we all our God with heart and hands and voices,
> who wondrous things hath done, in whom this world rejoices;
> who, from our mothers' arms, hath blessed us on our way
> with countless gifts of love, and still is ours today.

> O may this bounteous God through all our life be near us,
> with ever joyful hearts and blessed peace to cheer us;
> and keep us in God's grace, and guide us when perplexed,
> and free us from all ills in this world and the next.

> All praise and thanks to God, who reigns in highest heaven,
> to Father and to Son and Spirit now be given:
> the one eternal God, whom heaven and earth adore,

the God who was, and is, and shall be evermore.
                    Martin Rinkart; trans. Catherine Winkworth

Questions for Reflection

1. What narrative of gratitude can you tell in which God has rescued, delivered, or restored you when you could not do it for yourself? Describe what happened using the four stages illustrated by Psalm 30: *prosperity, dismay, complaint, resolution.*

2. Use another model provided by the Psalms to develop this narrative of thanks in response to God's action, perhaps even by writing out your own script or psalm:
   - follow the sequence of dire need, petition, rescue, thanks
   - focus on the verbs of God's power (Ps. 107)
   - answer the question "what shall I return to the Lord?" using first-person verbs (Ps. 116)

3. How does the rhetoric of the Psalms help us move beyond our rational and reasoned analysis of the way the world works, to a more gratitude-oriented understanding of God's intervention? How does this shift in understanding flip the categories of wise/foolish?

4. What cues can you use during the celebration of the Eucharist to engage it as an act of defiant gratitude over self-sufficiency?

Chapter 12

Spirit-Led Imagination

Reality Practiced in a Sub-Version

*T*he practice of faithful worship is more odd than we often take it to be. In recent time much of that oddness has been relinquished in the church, in a seductive attempt to be current, popular, alternative, or entertaining. Worship is an act of poetic imagination that aims to reconstrue the world. By imagination, it presents lived reality in images, figures, and metaphors that defy conventional structures of plausibility and that host alternative scenarios of reality that cut beyond our conventional perceptual field. This act of imagination that offers an alternative world is, perforce, a poetic act; that is, it is given in playful traces and sideways hints that do not conform to any of our usual categories of understanding or explanation. The practice of such poetic imagination is deeply rooted in old texts, old memories, and old practices; it nonetheless requires contemporary, disciplined, informed imagination to sustain alternative vision.

I will cite three mighty acts of poetic imagination in the Old Testament that are characteristic acts of worship to which the community repeatedly returns.

I

In the old poem in Exodus 15:21, Miriam and the other women, as they departed Egypt and began the journey into the wilderness and eventually to the land of promise, with tambourines sang:

> Sing to the LORD, for he has triumphed gloriously;
> horse and rider he has thrown into the sea.

This brief hymn exemplifies the way in which Israel does praise. It invites the community to sing to YHWH. It does not explain, because everyone knows. Everyone knows we have just witnessed an inexplicable triumphant act in the world, and everyone knows that it must be referred to the holy God who is creator of heaven and earth. Everyone knows that the only fitting response to such an awesome turn in the world is to sing, to offer deep-throated, lyrical, pre-rational exuberance to the giver of life. Miriam and the other women knew before the Wesleys what the Wesleys exhibited so well: that worship is a full, unqualified sense of glad abandonment of our life toward the giver of all life.

This little hymn gives reason for exuberance. YHWH has won a great victory. YHWH has destroyed Egyptian armaments and has overthrown the mighty imperial superpower. Miriam does not know how this happened and has no mandate to explain. Miriam's testimony is not a mechanical response to what happened. It is, rather, an act of deep imagination, for the overthrow of Pharaoh could be explained, as it has been by critical studies, on other grounds: there was a mighty wind, this was an escape of slaves, there was a lapse in state security, there was a dismissal of surplus labor. All that is of course possible, but no, says this worship leader, Miriam. She has imagined and construed the wonder differently, and at worship we will not pause over trivializing explanation. The event is miracle with marks of holy awe, and it must not be reduced to explanation. It is miracle that invites exuberance and dismay, whereas explanation invites control and management and no doubt another layer of committees.[1]

Well, as you might imagine, the hymnal committee (chaired by a man) transposed the spontaneous outburst of Miriam and the other women into a longer, more stable poem, the so-called Song of Moses in Exodus 15:1–18. That poetry begins with the attestation of Miriam:

> Then Moses and the Israelites sang this song to the LORD:
> "I will sing to the LORD, for he has triumphed gloriously;
>   horse and rider he has thrown into the sea."
>
> v. 1

It continues, by way of extrapolation, with more hymnic introduction (vv. 2–3). And then through poetic imagination it provides a narrative scenario of the death of Pharaoh. The community of emancipated slaves in generation after generation sing the song and celebrate the overthrow of whoever is the current pharaoh. We watch as the writers imagined the deathly power of Pharaoh and settled on a way to characterize the God of the wind who put tyranny to death:

> Pharaoh's chariots and his army he cast into the sea;
> his picked officers were sunk in the Red Sea.
> The floods covered them;
> they went down into the depths like a stone.
> Your right hand, O LORD, glorious in power—
> your right hand, O LORD, shattered the enemy.
> In the greatness of your majesty you overthrew your adversaries;
> you sent out your fury, it consumed them like stubble.
> At the blast of your nostrils the waters piled up,
> the floods stood up in a heap;
> the deeps congealed in the heart of the sea.
> The enemy said, "I will pursue, I will overtake,
> I will divide the spoil, my desire shall have its fill of them.
> I will draw my sword, my hand shall destroy them."
> You blew with your wind, the sea covered them;
> they sank like lead in the mighty waters.
>
> vv. 4–10

Nothing is explained. Everything stays hidden except the outcome. The outcome to which the narrative leads is that everything has been transformed!

The hymnal committee of course took liberties with Miriam's little verse. In canonical form it is not enough to cross the waters, a wonder of which Miriam had sung. The whole narrative must be told, because the narrative is the screen memory for all of faith in Israel. The slaves not only go out. They go in . . . to the land of promise. Thus, in verses 13–17, these ex-slaves are led "in your steadfast love," led through dangerous valleys of death amid Edomites and Moabites and Ammonites, those who did not subscribe to this act of imagination. In the song, the children of the exodus arrive safely in the land of promise:

> You brought them in and planted them on the mountain of your
> own possession,

the place, O LORD, that you made your abode,
the sanctuary, O LORD, that your hands have established.
v. 17

It was a long journey, and Israel would have many stories to tell of that journey. But the skeletal structure of Israel's imagination is now in place. The narrative that scripts this imagination is from slavery to safety, from death to life, from oppression to freedom; this story has countless variations and is endlessly resung, because the imaginative drama is always required in new circumstance.

The poem is symmetrical: verses 4–10 concerns the death of Pharaoh, who can be any face of brutalizing power; verses 13–17 tells of the arrival at well-being. In between these two units, we are offered a formula of incomparability, for no other god has been so allied with slaves:

Who is like you, O LORD, among the gods?
Who is like you, majestic in holiness,
awesome in splendor, doing wonders?
v. 11

It is YHWH, directly, immediately, whose great spirit of power has turned the world. The song can for that reason culminate with a great mantra of enthronement:

The LORD will reign forever and ever.
v. 18

There has been regime change. A new king is among us who has no brick quotas and no imperial palaces based on forced labor, and who offers a world covenantally arranged. It is no wonder that the men joined the women singing, precisely because "he shall reign forever and ever and ever."

So sang Miriam and so echoed Moses. They did not need to say it as they did. But they said it in this particular way, and this has become our way of speaking of a new rule of God in the earth, the realm of well-being that we regularly enact in worship. We regularly enact it in hope, defiance, and resolve. The song is an act of imagination that hopes an alternative, because the data is all against the song. The data indicates old management by alienating superpowers with brick quotas. But for this one moment, over and over, we refuse the data. We enter another zone of reality that must be expressed—not precisely, not didactically, but in raw exuberance about large nostrils of wind and kings sinking like lead, and populations seized with dread and then settlement and peace. We refuse to give in to the data of the day because we, like them, "desire a better country," a city that has been prepared for us (Heb. 11:16).

II

Of course, the lyrical rawness that is so indispensable for Miriam and Moses is not everywhere sustained. The raw specificity at the beginning is reshaped into more urbane poetry, rounded out to a fuller picture; but the tenacity of fidelity is fully sustained. So consider a third script of praise, the astonishing litany of Psalm 136.

This litany begins with a threefold invitation to "give thanks to YHWH" (vv. 1–3). It knows that the proper stance of Israel before God is one of gratitude, because YHWH is the generous giver of life for Israel and for all creation. Such thanks in Israel is liturgically constituted by material offerings accompanied by appropriate words.[2] Here we have only the words; thanks is constituted by public testimony that acknowledges YHWH as the giver of gifts and Israel as recipient. The psalm concludes with a like invitation to thank; only now YHWH is not named but is identified as "the God of heaven," that is, the presiding sovereign of all creatures and all gods.

Thus the psalm is framed by two calls of thanks, and between them the body of the psalm provides specific grounds of thanks as it recites YHWH's engagement in the world and on behalf of Israel (vv. 4–25). It turns out that every part of Israel's life evokes Israel's thanks. In Israel's interpretative imagination, everything that happens is read as a sign and signal of YHWH's abiding fidelity (*hesed*); the world and its historical processes are known to be saturated with divine constancy and stability. Thus the litany proceeds so that the response to every line, a reprise surely uttered by the community at worship, concerns YHWH's fidelity.

The body of the psalm begins with reference to YHWH's great work in creation:

> who alone does great wonders,
>> for his steadfast love endures forever;
> who by understanding made the heavens,
>> for his steadfast love endures forever;
> who spread out the earth on the waters,
>> for his steadfast love endures forever;
> who made the great lights;
>> for his steadfast love endures forever;
> the sun to rule over the day,
>> for his steadfast love endures forever;
> the moon and stars to rule over the night,
>> for his steadfast love endures forever.
>>   vv. 4–9

There follows a long litany (vv. 10–15) concerning the exodus deliverance, in a song not unlike Exodus 15, and then the conventional sequence of wilderness sojourn and entry into the land (vv. 16–22). The body of the psalm concludes with a wondrous summary in three parts:

> It is he who remembered us in our low estate,
>> for his steadfast love endures forever;
> and rescued us from our foes,
>> for his steadfast love endures forever;
> who gives food to all flesh,
>> for his steadfast love endures forever.
>>   vv. 23–25

In this conclusion, Israel remembers its abasement, surely a reference to exodus slavery, and acknowledges divine rescue (vv. 23–24). Surprisingly this is followed by a reference to the reliable food chain of creation (v. 25).

This psalmic imagination reflects a larger body of poetry. The reference to "low estate" recalls Psalm 123, which reflects on YHWH's transformative mercy from a context of contempt:

> As the eyes of servants
>> look to the hand of their master,
> as the eyes of a maid
>> to the hand of her mistress,

so our eyes look to the LORD our God,
    until he has mercy upon us.
Have mercy upon us, O LORD, have mercy upon us,
    for we have had more than enough of contempt.
Our soul has had more than its fill
    of the scorn of those who are at ease,
    of the contempt of the proud.

123:2–4

The reference to "food to all flesh," moreover, evokes the great creation hymns that celebrate the abundance of food:

These all look to you
    to give them their food in due season;
when you give to them, they gather it up;
    when you open your hand, they are filled with good things.

104:27–28

The eyes of all look to you,
    and you give them their food in due season.
You open your hand,
    satisfying the desire of every living thing.

145:15–16

All creation is pulsing with YHWH's faithfulness.

The world can be imagined differently. It can be imagined with
Thomas Hobbes as a war of each against all. It can be imagined
with Henry Kissinger as a world in which might makes right. It can
be imagined with Milton Friedman as a place of scarcity where we
compete for limited goods. It can be imagined with Tom Ridge (US
secretary of homeland security after 9/11) as a place of chaos, threat,
and risk. All such construals are possible and frequently enacted. But
not in Israel. Not in this world of worship. Israel reads and imagines
and celebrates otherwise, by appeal to its own remembered narrative
of constant fidelity, such constancy that evokes assured and unanx-
ious gratitude. (There are, to be sure, testimonies in Israel that con-
strue differently, but in this canonical recital the point is clear.) It is
evident that out of the materials of its experience and observation,
Israel is engaged in world making, so that Israel ends the psalm in a
safe place where gratitude is the appropriate response.

III

As Exodus 15 narrates the raw reality of victory and Psalm 136 styl-
izes that victory into a collage of affirmations, so my third example,
Psalm 107, at the same time (a) moves from grand communal affirmation to concrete lived experience, and (b) goes underneath glad
doxology to the vexations that mark every life in God's world.

Psalm 107 begins with a summons to thank, not unlike Psalm 136,
on the grounds that YHWH is "good" and that, as in Psalm 136, his
steadfast love endures forever. This is the baseline of faith and the
ground of gratitude:

> O give thanks to the LORD, for he is good,
>   for his steadfast love endures forever.
> Ps. 107:1

But this psalm goes further. It also identifies those who most readily and appropriately will give thanks:

> Let the redeemed of the LORD say so,
>   those he redeemed from trouble
> and gathered in from the lands,
>   from the east and from the west,
>   from the north and from the south.
> vv. 2–3

The ones who can make gestures of gratitude are the ones who have
been "redeemed from trouble." The reference could be to the oppression of Egypt, but the psalm will make clear that the invitation is
to all sorts of human persons. And the parallel refers to all those
"gathered," that is, returned from exile and displacement. The rhetoric of verse 3 is inclusive and pertains to all who have been brought
home, and all who had lived through God's generous homecoming.
The four-directional inclusion recalls Isaiah 43:6–7, wherein YHWH
seeks out the scattered:

> I will say to the north, "Give them up,"
>   and to the south, "Do not withhold;
> bring my sons from far away
>   and my daughters from the end of the earth—

> everyone who is called by my name,
>> whom I created for my glory,
>> whom I formed and made."

That rhetorical maneuver acknowledges the God of all gathering:

> Thus says the Lord GOD,
>> who gathers the outcasts of Israel,
> I will gather others to them
>> besides those already gathered.
>> Isa. 56:8

The ones who give thanks to YHWH are the ones who know YHWH's *hesed* firsthand.

Psalm 107:4–38 then lines out, in four case studies, some particular examples of those who have been alienated and restored. The content is remarkable because of its capacity to remember, recall, and characterize specific situations of distress.

The first case, characteristic of the fourfold stylized report, describes a situation of wanderers lost in the wilderness without resources:

> Some wandered in desert wastes,
>> finding no way to an inhabited town;
> hungry and thirsty,
>> their soul fainted within them.
>> vv. 4–5

But the Israelites know that a petition addressed to YHWH is the appropriate antidote to such dismay:

> Then they cried to the LORD in their trouble.
>> v. 6a

The remarkable movement of the rhetoric indicates that without pause or pondering of any kind, the deliverance of YHWH follows promptly upon petition:

> and he delivered them from their distress;
> he led them by a straight way,
>> until they reached an inhabited town.
>> vv. 6b–7

These two rhetorical elements state the substance of Israel's most elemental worship, namely, *cry in need* and divine *response of rescue*. While it will not be true in two subsequent cases I will mention, here the crisis has nothing to do with guilt. What counts is not guilt but need. Israel knew exactly what to do about desperate need, namely, to recognize one's own inadequacy and to turn to the fully adequate Lord.

In a complex and extensive discussion, Karl Barth has asserted that prayer in Christian tradition is "simply asking."[3] Barth continues to say that asking God is "the most genuine act of praise and thanksgiving and therefore worship." More than that, says Barth, "God does not act in the same way whether we pray or not." Prayer "exerts an influence upon God's action, even upon his existence."

Thus it is no surprise that the cry of the wilderness wanderers in their hunger and thirst is promptly answered with divine deliverance. This God hears and decisively responds to the need of Israel. Indeed, as Claus Westermann has shown, this structure of "cry-answer" or "cry-save" is the core plot of biblical faith and therefore the core claim of worship.[4] From the finite verbs "deliver" and "lead," Israel at worship—because of countless cases of concrete testimony—can generalize about God's *hesed*. The generalizing affirmation about YHWH, moreover, introduces the crucial term *niphel'oth* ("wonderful acts"), acts of transformation that defy explanation and belong in the peculiar category of miracle. No wonder this tightly drawn rhetoric concludes with a summons to thanks. The final verse of the unit returns to the beginning and reiterates the initial need, only now it is need satisfied:

> For he satisfies the thirsty,
> and the hungry he fills with good things.
> v. 9

Now the governing verbs are of a different sort: "satisfy," "fill." These terms, bespeaking the abundance of creation, are very different from the previous verbs—"deliver," "lead"—that attest historical activity. The four verbs together thus witness both to YHWH's disruptive rescue as redeemer and to YHWH's generous sustenance as creator.

The plot line of verses 4–9 provides a sketch of Israel's faith and surely a sequence of right worship: need, cry, rescue, thanks. That same plot line is reiterated in three additional case studies. In *Psalm 107:10–16*, the stylized sequence goes: need (vv. 10–12); cry (v. 13a); rescue (vv. 13b–14); response of thanks (v. 15); and a reprise of need resolved (v. 16). In the rescue of YHWH, the governing verbs are "save," "bring out," "break." And in the reprise it is "shatter," "cut," all verbs of forceful action. These verbs in sum constitute a "wonderful work" (miracle) that is sure to evoke thanks for the inexplicable gift of new life.

In *Psalm 107:17–22*, the plot is now familiar: need (vv. 17–18); cry (v. 19a); rescue (vv. 19b–20); and thanks (vv. 21–22). In the rescue, the verbs are "save," "send," "heal," "deliver"—thus a more extensive cluster of terms. The response of thanks is now more extended, having displaced any reprise from this episode.

Verse 21 reiterates the familiar formula of thanks for *hesed* and *niphel'oth*. Verse 22 indicates the enactment of thanks in cultic form. Now the thanks is not only verbal, but includes a thank-offering, a gift of material significance; and the gift is matched by telling, that is, by narrating the rescue from the crisis described in verses 17–19. Thus verse 22 reflects precisely a combination of "Word and sacrament."

The fourth case, in *Psalm 107:23–32*, is extended but still familiar: need (vv. 24–27); cry (v. 28a); rescue (vv. 28b–30); and thanks (vv. 31–32). Here the crisis is credited directly to YHWH; the storm that causes the trouble is a *niphel'oth* wrought by YHWH's command. The verbs of rescue include "bring out," "made still." The element of thanks is again extended in verse 32 to include extolment and praise in the midst of the congregation. In all these cases, the moment of miracle has been transposed into a stylized narrative, the purpose of which is to instruct, summon, and empower the congregation to participate in this world of miracles and of decisively answered prayer.

Psalm 107 concludes with two more generalized affirmations, more or less derivative from these case studies. In verses 33–38, YHWH is celebrated as the creator who turns rivers to deserts and fruitful land to waste, and who blesses the hungry with all the fruitfulness of creation. The rhetoric recalls Genesis 1. In 107:39–41, the rhetoric concerns social transformation in a way that reflects the Song of Hannah and anticipates the Song of Mary:

> When they are diminished and brought low
>   through oppression, trouble, and sorrow,
> he pours contempt on princes
>   and makes them wander in trackless wastes;
> but he raises up the needy out of distress,
>   and makes their families like flocks.

Nature is imagined as "creation," and history is imagined as an arena for YHWH's revolutionary activity. The psalm concludes with an invitation to wise discernment of this Yahwistic reality, the neglect of which leads to trouble; the final phrase, yet one more time, concerns the *hesed* of YHWH. All of these case studies attest concretely to the divine fidelity that is voiced in the liturgy of Psalm 136. I have taken time to consider three songs:

- Exodus 15, voiced by Miriam and then by Moses, is a *victory* song that plots Israel's way from slavery to the land of promise;
- Psalm 136 is a hymn that attests to *YHWH's fidelity* in every sphere of life;
- Psalm 107 is a song of thanksgiving that brings the fidelity of YHWH close to *concrete lived human experience*.

These highly stylized, self-aware poems are accomplishments of daring imagination that read out of and into lived experience. Every experience that is reported in Israel is understood with reference to YHWH, without whom the event would not be. I cite these cases to insist that Christian worship is an act of human imagination that voices, advocates, and insists upon a gospel perception of all lived reality. The substance of worship is to tell the story in the form of many smaller stories, all of them featuring YHWH as the key character, so that the contemporary congregation, many seasons later, may participate as directly as possible in a world of miraculous fidelity to which the text attests and that YHWH decisively inhabits.

I deliberately use the term "imagination" because I want to insist that such stylized narrative account is indeed a human construction. The poets put the words together in this particular way. The poets utilized this pattern of worship in order to reiterate and reenact this advocacy. Every time a pastor and a choir director pick hymns, the work is one of constructive imagination designed to lead the congregation in turn to imagine the world in a certain way. Much worship is informed by tradition and conventional practice, but those who construct such worship must commit an act of imagination in order to determine what is to be accented and to adapt the advocacy to the specificity of context.

Having said that, we inescapably must ask if it is all "made up," for the term "imagination" is a tricky one. In the community of faith, to "imagine" does not mean to "make up," but rather, to receive, entertain, and host images of reality that are outside the accepted given. If, however, we say "receive" images, then we may ask, "Receive from whom?" or "Receive for whom?" The answer is that what the psalmists and liturgists imagine and shape and offer is given by God's spirit, who bears witness. It is the spirit that has given Israel freedom to recognize and acknowledge YHWH as savior from slavery. It is the spirit that gives us eyes to see and selves to notice the recurring and constant fidelity of God. It is the spirit that cries out with us that lets us cry out and receive God's rescue. It is the spirit that moves in the faith of the community and in the artistry of the poet to give voice to the odd truth of our common life.

Or it may be put differently. When Peter confessed Jesus to be the Messiah, Jesus blessed Peter for his confession:

And Jesus answered him, "Blessed are you, Simon son of Jonah! For flesh and blood has not revealed this to you, but my Father in heaven." (Matt. 16:17)

So it is with all the great liturgic claims of the church and with the text from which these liturgic claims arise. It is not "flesh and blood" that has let us see these matters. It is rather the self-disclosing God, who has let Israel and the church see that the drama of fidelity is God's own act. Thus the God who is the subject of our testimony and our worship also discloses what we know of that truth. That spirit, moreover, has been present not only in the originary event and at the point of initiation, but also in our contemporary appropriation, in our interpretation, and in the imagination that makes contemporaneity possible. We may indeed say that worship is an act of spirit-led imagination.

But insofar as our worship is an act of spirit-led imagination that permits us to see and live differently, it is against the grain of dominant reality. Worship does not happen in a vacuum, but always in response to contexts. In the context of the North American church, worship that is spirit-led imagination is powerfully over and against dominant reality. One way to consider this interface is to ask what the contrary may be to each of our three texts:

1. In *Exodus 15:21*, and derivatively in verses 1–18, we see the joyous celebration of the overthrow of Pharaoh by the God who is incomparable in compassion and power. In the long stretch of the Bible, "Pharaoh" is not only a historical person, but a metaphor and symbol for all established power that seeks to organize the world against covenantal freedom, justice, and neighborliness.

But imagine the world of Pharaoh without this poem, without the incomparable God of freedom, justice, and neighborliness. Imagine that Pharaoh had never been overthrown, could not be challenged, and was never placed in jeopardy. Without this dangerous poetic imagination of worship, we have a world in which entrenched, oppressive power is guaranteed to last to perpetuity. Take away the poem and its worshiping practitioners, and the slaves are fated forever to brick quotas, reduced to silence without ever a moan or a groan of self-announcement. Take away the tambourines of Miriam, and we are left with an unchanging world of unbearable despair.

But of course that is the world that the dominant narrative of our time offers us. It believes that technological capacity, economic monopoly, and military mastery can keep the world the way it is forever. It believes that control of finance can keep wealth and poverty as they are, which places most social pathologies beyond redress. Once given that narrative of despair, oppressive interpersonal relationships are fated to last, because a heavy dose of authoritarianism maintains equilibrium and yields no change. At best we are left with shopping and entertainment in a world that is closed and fixed, stable without a chance for hope.

And then imagine that the congregation, in the wake of Miriam, begins to sing and dance and remember the overthrow of power. It

could have been Pharaoh, or it could have been Nebuchadnezzar
when we left exile:

> When the LORD restored the fortunes of Zion,
>   we were like those who dream.
> Then our mouth was filled with laughter,
>   and our tongue with shouts of joy;
> then it was said among the nations,
>   "The LORD has done great things for them."
> The LORD has done great things for us,
>   and we rejoiced.
>
> Ps. 126:1–3

Or it could have been the power of death when the church joined the
Easter laugh and signed on with the Lord of the Dance who has led
the dance since the days of Miriam.

2. *Psalm 136*, that highly stylized liturgy, offers a community of
remembering that recalls in some grandeur and close detail the wonders of creation and the dazzlement of exodus, sure that the incomparable God of freedom, justice, and neighborliness is directly at work
among us. And from this acute remembering, our singing community
has continued with what we take to be the long-term truth of God's
fidelity. This inventory of miracles shows God's fidelity to be concrete and accessible, and so the recital is sandwiched in the psalm by
thanks, thanks to YHWH for his goodness, thanks to YHWH who
is the Lord of Lords and God of Gods, thanks to the God of heaven,
whose miracles enfold all lived reality. Israel yields itself in gratitude, aware and glad to acknowledge that the decisive features of its
life of well-being are all a gift.

But imagine a world without this psalm and without the God
attested there. Imagine a group of people who no longer meet to sing
and dance and remember fidelity. In that world:

- Memory is lost and amnesia is the order of the day, forgetfulness
  that assumes that there were none before us and none to come
  after us, only us, free to use up all of creation—and its oil!—in
  our own extravagant way. Moses, of course, knows that affluence
  breeds amnesia and the loss of a grounding memory:

  > When you have eaten your fill and have built fine houses
  > and live in them, and when your herds and flocks have

> multiplied, and your silver and gold is multiplied, and all
> that you have is multiplied, then do not exalt yourself,
> forgetting the LORD your God, who brought you out of the
> land of Egypt. . . . Do not say to yourself, "My power and
> the might of my own hand have gotten me this wealth."
> But remember the LORD your God, for it is he who gives
> you power to get wealth, so that he may confirm his cove-
> nant that he swore to your ancestors, as he is doing today.
> (Deut. 8:12–14, 17–18)

Eat, enjoy, be full enough, forget enough, until we arrive at
a place where we no longer say, "This do in remembrance
of me," because the "me" of God has been overwhelmed in
a vacuum.

- Fidelity disappears in a large binge of self-indulgence. We no
  longer remember the faithful God; we no longer remember to
  imitate God in faithfulness; we no longer remember that fidelity
  is the coin of humanness. In place of fidelity come power and
  greed, cunning manipulation, and anxiety, because covenants
  are reduced to contracts and promises are only conveniences.
  And our humanness erodes.

- Where memory fails before amnesia and where fidelity gives way
  to self-indulgence, there will be no thanks, no acknowledgment
  that life is a gift; we are free to imagine it as an achievement
  or a possession. Where there is no gratitude, there will be no
  thank-offering, no giving of self, no Eucharist, that great meal
  of thanks. And where there is no sacrament that dramatizes the
  world as a mystery of abundance, life becomes sheer commodity,
  and human relations are reduced to market transactions. Matters
  we have traditionally understood as social goods—medical care
  and education, for example—now become tools of leverage in
  the service of greed.

The dominant culture all around is one of self-indulgence without
fidelity, manipulation without gratitude.

Then comes this little body of singers breaking out in Psalm 136.
The loud narrative of acquisitiveness is shattered and shown to be
false. The powers of manipulation and monopoly are broken. The
singing itself is a dangerous protest of dissent from the dominant

culture that does not sing, for everything is reduced to formulae; but then this body sings its spirit-led alternative.

3. In *Psalm 107* we have four cases of human disaster and misery, lost in the wilderness, abandoned in prison, sick and without appetite, nearly lost at sea. In that highly stylized account, every troubled person becomes a person able to cry out in need and address pain to God. It turns out to be no surprise that God in fidelity answers, reassures, and makes transformation possible. But the trigger in each case is the cry, the capacity to find voice, the sense of entitlement that pain may speak to power and insist upon redress. For that reason, our worship must not be too happy, too well ordered, or too symmetrically serene, for at the heart of our worship is asking in need, being answered and taken seriously.

But imagine a world without Psalm 107, with no one to sing this great song of thanks, no acknowledgment of rescue grounded in fidelity, no communal awareness that life consists in situations of distress, and, above all, no recognition of the cry of distress that sets in motion the divine mystery of rescue. Imagine a world without the public processing of pain, without the insistent sense of entitlement that we deserve better. Imagine a world cold and numb to human pain. Imagine a world totally silenced, no prayers uttered, no hopes voiced, no hosting of the human condition and, consequently, no miracles of newness or healing.

The dominant culture and its narrative account of reality go a long way toward such silence. Just suck it up and get on with your life! If you are in trouble, it is your fault, so get with the program. At most, those in deep need become only a forgotten statistic; "compassionate conservatism" becomes a retaliatory regression with no answering of human community or compassion, but only slanderous impatience toward those without power to save themselves.

And then, right in the midst of such systemic silencing, the congregation breaks out in Psalm 107. It recalls disasters, remembers rescues, and gives thanks. In the center of that remembering is the cry, the urge and energy and authority of out-loud pain that causes the world to regroup in new ways.[5] In giving voice to old distresses resolved by the mercy of God, the congregation invites those in present distress to find voice and hope that may yet again move God to act.

The dominant version of reality in antineighborly late capitalism moves along without these great texts:

- goes *without Exodus 15*, and so imagines that oppressive power is forever;
- goes *without Psalm 136*, with nothing of fidelity, and so gives no thanks;
- goes *without Psalm 107*, and ends in silence that crushes the human spirit.

All of us are to some extent practitioners of this dominant version of reality. It comes at us in many forms; if we conform to that dominant voice of reality, we may receive its surface gifts of well-being and security for a while. There is enough truth in the dominant version for it to maintain credibility, but only for a while![6]

There is, however, a countertruth that surfaces in Christian worship. It is a small counterpoint without great voice or muscle. It has been a minority perspective for a very long time. The ones who practice the counterpoint know well that ours is not and will not be a dominant voice. It is a sub-version of reality, one that sounds beneath the loud sounds of the dominant version, one that flies low beneath the radar surveillance of the dominant version.

This evangelical sub-version of reality lives in delicate tension with the dominant version. It sometimes has aspiration to become the dominant version, as in many of the psalms that make sweeping liturgical claims for the God featured in this sub-version. Thus, Psalm 117:1 imagines all nations celebrating this compassionate sovereign. And Psalm 96:10 lines out a message of assurance to all nations in the name of this monarch newly come to power.

But in fact the sub-version is a poetic, elusive, delicate alternative, even while the dominant voice of reality prevails in its facts on the ground. Our liturgical practice acknowledges the resilience of the dominant version of reality, but we reiterate yet again the sub-version in the liturgy as a viable, credible, choosable alternative. Thus, the community

- *offers Exodus 15* as an alternative to the claim that oppressive power is forever;

- *offers Psalm 136* as an alternative of fidelity to a social vision of greed;
- *offers Psalm 107* as an alternative cry to a social coercion of enforced silence.

In every such liturgical utterance, act, and gesture, this sub-version of reality intends to subvert dominant versions, to expose them as inadequate if not false, and to empower the community to reengage reality according to this sub-version.

This delicate tension between dominant and sub-version, I believe, is the true character of worship. The claims made in the sub-version, claims such as "Christ is risen," are a deeply felt, eagerly offered truth. And yet in its very utterance the community at worship knows that the facts on the ground, the data at hand, contradict this and give evidence that the odor of death is still very much in play. It will not do for the church to become cynical and give in to the dominant vision. But it also will not do for the church to become excessively romantic about its sub-version and so to imagine its dominance. Rather, I believe that the worshiping community must live knowingly and elusively in this tension, not cynical, not romantic, but wise and innocent (Matt. 10:16), always engaged in negotiation between subclaim and the world the way we find it.

The task and goal of worship, accompanied by education and pastoral care, is to move our lives from the dominant version of reality to the sub-version, so that our old certitudes will have been subverted by the work of the spirit. Judged by the dominant version, life in the sub-version is vulnerable and foolish and exposed. But the sub-version in the end cannot be judged by the dominant version. In the end, it is judged by the truth of the gospel, by the reality of God whom we attest, and by the truth of our own lives in the image of that God. We are endlessly seduced out of that truth by the dominant version, and so we return to worship to recite and receive this sub-version that is the truth of our life and of the world.

In the Old Testament, the psalms vigorously and without apology line out that sub-version and make a claim against the data at hand (for a familiar example, see Ps. 23). In the New Testament, none more eloquently lined out the truth of the sub-version than Paul (see 1 Cor. 1:18–31; Rom. 4:16–17; 8:37–39).

We leave the hearing and speaking of the sub-version and reenter the world that has not yet come to this alternative. We make our way in compromise and timidity, fear and trembling. But then we enter gladly into the voice of the sub-version, yet again, sure of our true home and our real identity:

> O come, let us sing to the LORD;
>> let us make a joyful noise to the rock of our salvation!
> Let us come into his presence with thanksgiving;
>> let us make a joyful noise to him with songs of praise!
> For the LORD is a great God,
>> and a great King above all gods.
> In his hand are the depths of the earth;
>> the heights of the mountains are his also.
> The sea is his, for he made it,
>> and the dry land, which his hands have formed.
> O come, let us worship and bow down,
>> let us kneel before the LORD, our Maker!
> For he is our God,
>> and we are the people of his pasture.
>
> Ps. 95:1–7a

Questions for Reflection

1. What are the "old texts, old memories, and old practices" that speak most deeply to your poetic imagination during worship and point toward the alternative vision of God? How do they correlate to the countertruths presented in these three passages?

   - Exodus 15's alternative to the claim that oppressive power is forever
   - Psalm 136's alternative of fidelity to a social vision of greed
   - Psalm 107's alternative cry to a social coercion of enforced silence

2. How does the flow of Christian worship follow the sequence sketched out in Psalm 107:4–9: *need, cry, rescue, thanks*? What discrete elements of worship contain echoes of that overarching sequence within them? What are some of the smaller stories being

told in your community that help your congregation participate in the world of God's miraculous fidelity?

3. Whose voices are loudest right now in describing the world through the dominant narrative of "antineighborly late capitalism," with its celebration of established power, amnesia, anxiety, self-sufficiency, and greed?

4. What role do the Psalms play in your congregation's worship? When or how are they employed—or how could they be used more fully—in the crucial task of helping worshipers move from the dominant narrative to the Bible's astonishing sub-version of reality?

Acknowledgments

Chapters 1, 3, 6, 7, and 11 include material from Walter Brueggemann, *From Whom No Secrets Are Hid: Introducing the Psalms*, ed. Brent A. Strawn (Louisville, KY: Westminster John Knox, 2014). Used by permission.

Chapter 2 includes revised material from Walter Brueggemann, *Israel's Praise: Doxology against Idolatry and Ideology* (Philadelphia: Fortress, 1988). Used by permission.

Chapter 4 includes revised material from Walter Brueggemann, "Praise and the Psalms: A Politics of Glad Abandonment, Part I," *The Hymn: A Journal of Congregational Song* 43/3 (July 1992): 14–19, ©1992, The Hymn Society in the United States and Canada. Used by permission.

Chapter 5 includes revised material from Walter Brueggemann, "Praise and the Psalms: A Politics of Glad Abandonment, Part II," *The Hymn: A Journal of Congregational Song* 43/4 (October 1992): 14–18, ©1992, The Hymn Society in the United States and Canada. Used by permission.

Chapter 8 includes revised material from Walter Brueggemann, "The Formfulness of Grief," *Interpretation* 31, no. 3 (1977): 263–75. Reprinted by permission of SAGE Publications.

Chapter 9 includes revised material from Walter Brueggemann, "The Costly Loss of Lament," *Journal for the Study of the Old Testament* 36 (1986): 57–71. Reprinted by permission of SAGE Publications.

Chapters 10 and 12 include material from Walter Brueggemann, *Mandate to Difference: An Invitation to the Contemporary Church* (Louisville, KY: Westminster John Knox, 2007). Used by permission.

Notes

EDITOR'S INTRODUCTION
1. See in particular Walter Brueggemann, *From Whom No Secrets Are Hid: Introducing the Psalms*, ed. Brent A. Strawn (Louisville, KY: Westminster John Knox, 2014). Note especially the collected bibliographies at the end of *From Whom No Secrets Are Hid* for lists of Brueggemann's work on the Psalms and on specific psalms.

CHAPTER 2: PRAISE AS A CONSTITUTIVE ACT
1. See Geoffrey Wainwright, "The Praise of God in the Theological Reflection of the Church," *Interpretation* 39 (1985): 39.
2. Sigmund Mowinckel, *Psalmenstudien*, 6 vols. (Amsterdam: Schippers, 1961). See also his later work, Sigmund Mowinckel, *The Psalms in Israel's Worship*, 2 vols. (Nashville: Abingdon; Oxford: Basil Blackwell & Mott, 1962).
3. Mowinckel, *Psalmenstudien*, vol. 2: *Das Thronbesteigungsfest Jahwäs und der Ursprung der Eschatologie* (Amsterdam: Schippert, 1961 [1922]).
4. See Aubrey Johnson, *Sacral Kingship in Ancient Israel* (Cardiff: University of Wales Press, 1967).
5. Mowinckel, *Thronbesteigungsfest*, 226–27 and passim.
6. On the meaning of myth in the context of cult, see Sigmund Mowinckel, *Religion and Cult: The Old Testament and the Phenomenology of Religion*, trans. John F. X. Sheehan, ed. K. C. Hanson (Eugene, OR: Cascade, 2012), 92–97.
7. For an introduction to the sociological and anthropological aspects of cult, see James D. Shaughnessy, ed., *The Roots of Ritual* (Grand Rapids: Eerdmans, 1973).
8. Mowinckel, *Thronbesteigungsfest*, 19.
9. Mowinckel, *Thronbesteigungsfest*, 21.
10. Mowinckel, *Thronbesteigungsfest*, 22.
11. On the epistemological crisis, see Langdon Gilkey, *Society and the Sacred* (New York: Crossroad, 1981). In a very different mode, see the comments of Theo.

Wilvliet in *A Place in the Sun* (Maryknoll, NY: Orbis, 1985), 25–41, on the epistemological break reflected in liberation hermeneutics.

12. On the shift in scholarly method, see Robert Polzin, *Moses and the Deuteronomist* (New York: Seabury, 1980), chap. 1.

13. On the notion of continuing creation, see Langdon Gilkey, *Maker of Heaven and Earth* (Garden City, NY: Doubleday & Co., 1959), 257 and passim; and Jürgen Moltmann, *God in Creation* (San Francisco: Harper & Row, 1985), 206–14.

14. On the "image of God" as the way in which human persons participate in God's creative activity, see Wolfhart Pannenberg, *Anthropology in Theological Perspective* (Philadelphia: Westminster, 1985). Note esp. chaps. 4, 7, and 8 on the interplay of imagination, formation of culture, and development of institutions, under the rubric "The Shared World."

15. Peter L. Berger and Thomas Luckmann, *The Social Construction of Reality* (Garden City, NY: Doubleday & Co., 1966).

16. Berger and Luckmann, *Social Construction*, 21.

17. Berger and Luckmann, *Social Construction*, 51.

18. Berger and Luckmann, *Social Construction*, 51.

19. Berger and Luckmann write of "reality" the way Mowinckel does "world," in quotation marks. They say, "The philosopher is driven to decide where the quotation marks are in order and where they may safely be omitted, that is, to differentiate between valid and invalid assertions about the world. This the sociologist cannot do. Logically, if not stylistically, he is stuck with the quotation marks" (Berger and Luckmann, *Social Construction*, 2). See Alfred Schutz and Thomas Luckmann, *The Structures of the Life-World* (Evanston, IL: Northwestern University Press, 1973), for a normative characterization of the notion of "lifeworld."

20. Peter L. Berger, *The Sacred Canopy* (Garden City, NY: Doubleday & Co., 1969), 40–41.

21. On the study of narrative and its importance for theology, see David Tracy, *The Analogical Imagination* (New York: Crossroad, 1981), 275–87. See esp. his comprehensive note (p. 296, n. 81).

22. Robert Kegan, *The Evolving Self* (Cambridge: Harvard University Press, 1982), 11.

23. Roy Schafer, *Language and Insight* (New Haven, CT: Yale University Press, 1978).

24. Schafer, *Language and Insight*, 18.

25. Paul Pruyser, *The Play of Imagination* (New York: International Universities Press, 1983).

26. Pruyser, *Play of Imagination*, 65. See also Walter Brueggemann, "The Third World of Evangelical Imagination," *Horizons in Biblical Theology* 8, no. 2 (1986): 61–84.

27. Gordon D. Kaufman, *God the Problem* (Cambridge: Harvard University Press, 1972); *The Theological Imagination* (Philadelphia: Westminster, 1981); and *Theology for a Nuclear Age* (Philadelphia: Westminster, 1985).

28. On rendering God, see Dale Patrick, *The Rendering of God in the Old Testament* (Philadelphia: Fortress, 1981). Note esp. his utilization of the insights of Hans Frei.

29. Kaufman, *God the Problem*, 85.

30. Indeed, Kaufman (*Theological Imagination*, 127) concedes that there is "a point where contemporary theology must—unavoidably—live out of tradition." See Kaufman's own appeal to the tradition in "Some Theological Emphases of the Early Swiss Anabaptists," *Mennonite Quarterly Review* 35 (1951): 75–99.

31. See Bernhard W. Anderson, *Creation in the Old Testament* (Philadelphia: Fortress, 1984), 14–21.

32. Amos N. Wilder, in *Jesus' Parables and the War of Myths: Essays in Imagination in Scripture* (Philadelphia: Fortress, 1982), has argued that each such world of literary creation competes with other worlds and so polemicizes against them.

33. See Sallie McFague, *Metaphorical Theology* (Philadelphia: Fortress, 1982).

34. Karen Lebacqz, *Professional Ethics: Power and Paradox* (Nashville: Abingdon, 1985), 119–20.

CHAPTER 4: PRAISE AND THE PSALMS: A POLITICS OF GLAD ABANDONMENT, PART ONE

1. Most helpful beginning points for this study are Daniel W. Hardy and David F. Ford, *Praising and Knowing God* (Philadelphia: Westminster, 1985), and Patrick D. Miller Jr., *Interpreting the Psalms* (Philadelphia: Fortress, 1986), 64–78. See also Patrick D. Miller Jr., "In Praise and Thanksgiving," *Theology Today* 45 (July 1988): 180–88.

2. For a helpful understanding of sacraments as an alternative construal of all of life, see Robert L. Browning and Roy A. Reed, *The Sacraments in Religious Education and Liturgy* (Birmingham, AL: Religious Education Press, 1985).

3. The general mode of poetic as I use it here opposes Enlightenment modes of technical reason that seek in principle to eliminate ambiguity. The programmatic elimination of ambiguity eliminates as well the possibility of transformation. On such a notion of the poetic, see Walter Brueggemann, *Finally Comes the Poet: Daring Speech for Proclamation* (Minneapolis: Fortress, 1989).

4. For further discussion and elaboration of this point, see chap. 9 below.

5. Claus Westermann, *Praise and Lament in the Psalms* (Atlanta: John Knox, 1981).

6. Westermann, *Praise and Lament*, esp. 272–80.

7. On this theme in the Bible, see Robert Davidson, *The Courage to Doubt: Exploring an Old Testament Theme* (Philadelphia: Trinity Press International, 1983).

8. See Dietrich Ritschl, *The Logic of Theology: A Brief Account of the Relation between Basic Concepts in Theology* (Philadelphia: Fortress, 1987), 15–27; James A. Scherer, "Missiological Naming: Who Shall I Say Sent Me?" in *Our Naming of God; Problems and Prospects of God-Talk Today*, ed. Carl E. Braaten (Minneapolis:

Fortress, 1989), 111–25, and Lesslie Newbigin, *The Gospel in a Pluralistic Society* (Grand Rapids: Eerdmans, 1989), 127, 227.

9. Concerning the Sabbath, Matitiahu Tsevat, *The Meaning of the Book of Job and Other Biblical Studies: Essays on the Literature arid Religion of the Hebrew Bible* (New York: KTAV, 1980), 48, writes, "Every seventh day the Israelite renounces his autonomy and affirms God's dominion over him." The renouncing of autonomy "is a parallel to ceding life over to God." The time of Sabbath seeks to do what the act of praise also does. Both acts, praise and Sabbath, break with the ideology of mastery.

10. For a fuller exposition of these themes, see Walter Brueggemann, "The Psalms as Prayer," *Reformed Liturgy & Music* 23 (Winter 1989): 13–26.

11. See James L. Mays, "Worship, World, and Power: An Interpretation of Psalm 100," *Interpretation* 23 (July 1969): 315–30.

12. On this monotheizing tendency, see James A. Sanders, "Adaptable for Life: The Nature and Function of Canon," in *Magnalia Dei: The Mighty Acts of God*, ed. Frank Moore Cross et al. (Garden City, NY: Doubleday & Co., 1976), 531–60.

13. On praise in relation to idolatry and ideology, see Walter Brueggemann, *Israel's Praise: Doxology against Idolatry and Ideology* (Philadelphia: Fortress, 1988), esp. chap. 4. More generally, see Pablo Richard et al., *The Idols of Death and the God of Life: A Theology* (Maryknoll, NY: Orbis, 1983).

14. On the theses of Marx, see David McLellan, *The Thought of Karl Marx: An Introduction* (London: Macmillan, 1971), 22.

15. On the notion of rhetoric as guerilla warfare, see Amos Niven Wilder, *Theopoetic: Theology and the Religious Imagination* (Philadelphia: Fortress, 1976), 28.

16. On the phrase, see Martin Buber, *Moses: The Revelation and the Covenant* (Atlantic Highlands, NJ: Humanities Press International, 1988), 75. For a commentary on this notion of historiography, see Emil Fackenheim, *God's Presence in History* (New York: Harper & Row, 1972), 8–14, and Walter Brueggemann, *Abiding Astonishment: Psalms, Modernity and the Making of History* (Louisville, KY, Westminster/John Knox, 1991).

17. Jon D. Levenson, *Creation and the Persistence of Evil: The Jewish Drama of Divine Omnipotence* (San Francisco: Harper & Row, 1988), has commented on regions of reality where life is still under severe adjudication.

18. On praise as an enactment of the gospel, see Walter Brueggemann, *Israel's Praise*, 30–38. Praise is the establishment of the *basar* ("good news") of God's governance.

19. Karl Barth, *Church Dogmatics*, III/3 (Edinburgh: T. & T. Clark, 1961), 289–368, speaks of the continuing power of "nothingness." Levenson, *Creation and the Persistence of Evil*, 139, writes of the "fragile lordship" of God in the world.

20. The pairing of the newspaper or an inventory of our own lives as evidence that the gospel is not yet fully established forms a nice contrast to the positive argument of Kant concerning the "starry heavens above and the moral law within." Whereas Kant took these points as a basis for ethical affirmation, the contemporary inclination is much more to accent the negativities.

21. On inutility, see Jacques Ellul, *The Politics of God & the Politics of Man* (Grand Rapids: Eerdmans, 1972), 190–99, for what he calls a "Meditation on Inutility." Concerning such inutility, Karl Barth, *Wolfgang Amadeus Mozart* (Grand Rapids: Eerdmans, 1986), 37–38, writes of Mozart's work: "Mozart's music is not, in contrast to that of Bach, a message, and not, in contrast to that of Beethoven, a personal confession. He does not reveal in his music any doctrine and certainly not himself. The discoveries ostensibly made in both these directions, especially in his later works, seem to me artificial and not very illuminating. Mozart does not wish to say anything: he just sings and sounds. Thus he does not force anything on the listener, does not demand that he make any decisions or take any positions; he simply leaves him free. Doubtless the enjoyment he gives begins in our accepting that. On one occasion he called death man's true best friend, and he thought daily of death, as his works plainly reveal. But he does not dwell on it unduly; he merely lets us discover it—precisely in that humility in which he himself is, so to speak, only the instrument with which he allows us to hear what he hears: what surges at him from God's creation, what rises in him, and must proceed from him."

CHAPTER 5: PRAISE AND THE PSALMS: A POLITICS OF GLAD ABANDONMENT, PART TWO

1. On this grouping of psalms as a conclusion, see Gerald Henry Wilson, *The Editing of the Hebrew Psalter*, SBL Dissertation Series 76 (Chico, CA: Scholars Press, 1985), 189–94, 225–26. See also Walter Brueggemann, "Bounded by Obedience and Praise: The Psalms as Canon," *Journal for the Study of the Old Testament* 50 (1991): 63–92.

2. On this psalm, see Walter Brueggemann, *The Message of the Psalms* (Minneapolis: Augsburg, 1984), 28–31.

3. Anthony R. Ceresko, "Psalm 149: Poetry, Themes (Exodus and Conquest), and Social Function," *Biblica* 67 (1986): 177–94.

4. On "violence" presented as an act of obedience to YHWH, see Walter Brueggemann, *Revelation and Violence: A Study in Contextualization* (Milwaukee: Marquette University Press, 1986).

5. Sean E. McEvenue, "Afterword," in *Lonergan's Hermeneutics: Its Development and Application*, ed. Sean E. McEvenue and Ben F. Meyer (Washington, DC: The Catholic University of America Press, 1989), 160, writes: "The liturgy returns to these texts as an occasion for the faithful to hear, to encounter and to join. Scripture is primarily for conversion, not for doctrine—for foundations, not for truths. The faithful today, who understand their faith through a system of doctrines and within a complex culture evolved beyond anything that biblical authors could have imagined, still return to these normative texts and stances in order to check the direction of the evolving and to renew vitality. Theologians return to the Old Testament to form their imagination and to motivate their research, not to answer their questions. The theologian articulates contemporary questions about God and world that arise precisely within this biblically formed and motivated imagination."

6. George Herbert, "Providence," in *The Life and Writings of the Rev. George Herbert: With the Synagogue* (Lowell, MA: George Woodward, 1834), 192–93 (emphasis added).

7. Daniel W. Hardy and David F. Ford, *Praising and Knowing God* (Philadelphia: Westminster, 1985), 142.

8. Gene Lees, *Meet Me at Jim and Andy's: Jazz Musicians and Their World* (New York: Oxford University Press, 1990).

9. This list of praising creatures is from Psalm 104. It is a motif echoed in the poem of George Herbert.

10. Cf. Eccl. 3:1–8, which reflects situations of liminality in which praise has power to transform and renew.

CHAPTER 6: DOXOLOGY: THE CREATOR TOYS WITH MONSTER CHAOS

1. Karl Barth, *Church Dogmatics*, III/3 (Edinburgh: T. & T. Clark, 1961), 291–92.

CHAPTER 8: THE FORMFULNESS OF GRIEF

1. This chapter seeks to work out some implications of a previous statement, "From Hurt to Joy, from Death to Life," *Interpretation* 28 (1974): 3–19; and Claus Westermann, "The Role of the Lament in the Theology of the Old Testament," *Interpretation* 28 (1974): 20–38.

2. See the summary statements of Hans Joachim Kraus, *Psalms 1–59* (Minneapolis: Augsburg, 1988), and Claus Westermann, "The Structure and History of Lament in the Old Testament," in *Praise and Lament in the Psalms* (Atlanta: John Knox, 1981), 165–213. More specifically on the elements of the standard form, see Westermann, "Structure and History," 170; Kraus, *Psalms 1–59*, 48–49; and Erhard Gerstenberger, "The Psalms," in *Old Testament Form Criticism*, ed. John H. Hayes, Trinity University Monograph Series in Religion 2 (San Antonio: Trinity University Press, 1974), 200. The fullest discussion we have is that of Westermann, *The Praise of God in the Psalms* (Richmond: John Knox, 1965). The enumerations of elements differ in detail but agree in the primary components.

3. See Hans Schmidt, *Das Gebet der Angeklagten im Alten Testament*, Beihefte zur Zeitschrift für die alttestamentliche Wissenschaft 49 (Giessen: Alfred Töpelmann, 1928). More recent study has sought to be more precise. Cf. Lienhard Delekat, *Asylie und Schutzorakel am Zionheiligtum* (Leiden: E. J. Brill, 1967); and Walter Beyerlin, *Die Rettung der Bedrängten in den Feindpsalmen der Einzelnen auf institutionelle Zusammenhänge untersucht*, Forschungen zur Religion und Literatur des Alten und Neuen Testaments 99 (Göttingen: Vandenhoeck & Ruprecht, 1970). Each of these hypotheses presumes a major stress on the relation of the Psalms to the Jerusalem temple. See Gerstenberger, "Psalms," 203.

4. Westermann, *Praise of God*.

5. Erhard Gerstenberger, *Der bittende Mensch: Bittritual und Klagelied des Einzelnen im Alten Testament*, Wissenschaftliche Monographien zum Alten und

Neuen Testament 51 (Neukirchen-Vluyn: Neukirchener Verlag, 1980). For a largely conciliar but less sociological treatment of lament in Elihu's speeches, see James F. Ross, "Job 33:14–30: The Phenomenology of Lament," *Journal of Biblical Literature* 94 (1975): 38–46.

6. Rainer Albertz, *Weltschöpfung und Menschenschöpfung*, Calwer Theologische Monographien 3 (Stuttgart: Calwer, 1974); see 171–72 for a summary of his thesis. See Rolf Rendtorff, "Die theologische Stellung des Schöpfungsglaubens bei Deuterojesaja," *Zeitschrift für Theologie und Kirche* 51 (1954): 3–13. Focus on the small group or smaller unit is important to Gerstenberger's earlier study, *Wesen und Herkunft des apodiktischen Rechts*, Wissenschaftliche Monographien zum Alten und Neuen Testament 20 (Neukirchen-Vluyn: Neukirchener Verlag, 1965). The movement toward the smaller unit reflects a general shift in Old Testament studies away from the hegemony of the Jerusalem-covenant renewal hypothesis. For the practice of ministry, there is room here to consider smaller units as centers of rehabilitation.

7. See Peter Berger, *The Sacred Canopy* (Garden City, NY: Doubleday & Co., 1969); Thomas Luckmann, *The Invisible Religion* (New York, Macmillan, 1967); and Berger and Luckmann, *The Social Construction of Reality* (Baltimore: Penguin, 1966).

8. Robert Merton has provided a useful definition of anomie (*Social Theory and Social Structure* [Glencoe, IL: Free Press, 1957], 162). I have used both terms, *anomie* and *chaos*, to affirm both dimensions: the crisis is mythic, but it is also psychic-social.

9. Westermann concludes: "In the investigation of all the LI [Psalms of Lament of the Individual] of the Old Testament, I found to my astonishment that there are no Psalms which do not progress beyond petition and lament" (*Praise of God*, 74). Terence Fretheim has called my attention to Psalm 88 as a possible exception. That, however, does not detract greatly from the importance of Westermann's observation.

10. Abraham Heschel has introduced the notion of the pathos of God into our awareness (*The Prophets* [New York: Harper & Row, 1962]). More recently the pathos of God and the apathy of modern persons with a technological consciousness have become important to theology. See Jürgen Moltmann, *The Crucified God* (New York: Harper & Row, 1974), 267–90; M. Douglas Meeks, "The 'Crucified God' and the Power of Liberation" (paper read at the American Academy of Religion, 1974), 31–43; and Dorothy Sölle, *Suffering* (Philadelphia: Fortress, 1975), 36–59. In a different context, see Elie Wiesel, *Ani Maamin* (New York: Random House, 1974). It is likely that devotion to the apathy of God has led to the purging of laments from the worship and consciousness of the church.

11. See the comments of Westermann, "Role of Lament," 26–27, on lament as a bold form of protest. Sölle, *Suffering*, 70–86, has shrewdly observed that the lament form is an important step from apathy to affirmation. The lament form itself is a linguistic act that redefines experience. See Lothar Perlitt, "Anklage und Freispruch Gottes," *Zeitschrift für Theologie und Kirche* 69 (1972): 290–303.

12. Gerstenberger suggests that a lament "bemoans a tragedy which cannot be reversed, while a complaint entreats God for help in the midst of tribulation"

("Jeremiah's Complaints," *Journal of Biblical Literature* 82 [1963]: 405n50). The former accepts the way the situation is, and the latter insists and expects that it will be changed. Though Gerstenberger does not do so, perhaps it can be argued that a lament is used by the apathetic who do not believe in a future, while those with pathos refuse to accept what is, and so they complain for change.

13. Gerstenberger has noted the future expectation in the lament of Israel: "Every lament of Israel hopes in a breakthrough, even if it comes in death or degenerates into self-curse. It presumes, against all appearances, on the help of Yahweh. An answer to the lament, as it could come forth in worship, meant fulfillment of the petition" ("Der klagende Mensch," in *Probleme biblischer Theologie*, ed. Hans Walter Wolff [Munich: Chr. Kaiser Verlag, 1971], 72). Cf. Sölle, *Suffering*, 68–70, on mute suffering. The first step is to restore the speech of freedom. And see Alfons Deissler, "Das Israel der Psalmen als Gottesvolk der Hoffenden," in *Die Zeit Jesu*, ed. G. Bornkamm and K. Rahner (Basel: Herder, 1970), 15–37, esp. 29ff.

14. Westermann, "Role of Lament," 30.

15. Exclusive attention will be given to Kübler-Ross's most important study, *On Death and Dying* (New York: Macmillan, 1969). I regard her subsequent work as less germane to this study and in any case more problematic. Reference should be made to the earlier and parallel discernment of such formfulness by Granger Westberg, *Good Grief* (Philadelphia: Fortress, 1962). Although religiously oriented, he also stayed exclusively with psychological categories of interpretation.

16. Lionel Whiston Jr. has reminded me that modernity also has its forms. But the ideology behind them is that they are accidents or conveniences rather than shapers of experience. As a result, modernity leaves us with the notion that the shape of experience does not matter or with a sense of the shapelessness of experience that prevents it from being experienced at all. Only forms let experience be experienced communally and meaningfully; formlessness must lead to apathy. See Sölle, who sees the interrelatedness of inoperative speech, banal optimism, and blind worship of the status quo (*Suffering*, 36–41). Presumed formlessness surely means the end of human freedom.

17. Kübler-Ross, *Death and Dying*, 38.

18. Westermann, *Praise of God*, 75, has most helpfully structured the lament as movement from petition to praise: "In my opinion, this fact that in the Psalms of the Old Testament there is no, or almost no, such thing as 'mere' lament and petition shows conclusively the polarity between praise and petition in the Psalms. The cry to God is here never one-dimensional, without tension. It is always somewhere in the middle between petition and praise. By nature it cannot be *mere* petition or lament, but is always underway from supplication to praise."

19. See Robert Jay Lifton and Eric Olson, *Living and Dying* (New York: Praeger, 1974); Lifton, *Boundaries* (New York: Random House, 1969).

20. Kübler-Ross, *Death and Dying*, 50–51.

21. See, again, Gerstenberger's comment that in Israel the speech is most often hopeful complaint and not resigned moaning. Israel's lack of laments is not

accidental. The covenantal lifeworld of Israel made such resignation inappropriate because YHWH can and does intrude to transform.

22. Israel's capacity to say "Thou" is decisive both for the form and for its history. Martin Buber reports an old rabbinic song focused on "Thou." See Hendrich Ott, *God* (Richmond: John Knox, 1974), 87; and H. W. Beck, *Weltformel contra Schöpfungsglaube* (Zurich: Theologischen Verlag, 1972), 209. Hans Walter Wolff, in an oral exegesis of Jonah 4, observed that Jonah's problem was his preoccupation with "I" at the expense of "Thou." Israel's covenantal speech kept "Thou" at the center of consciousness.

23. Kübler-Ross, *Death and Dying*, 70; see 68 and 81.

24. See Berger on the meaning of world-maintenance by the management of symbols (*Sacred Canopy*, 29–51).

25. See Westermann, *Praise of God*, 80; and Gerstenberger, "Der klagende Mensch," 72.

26. See Roy Branson, "Is Acceptance a Denial of Death?" *The Christian Century* 92 (May 7, 1975): 464–68, and Robert M. Herhold, "Kübler-Ross and Life After Death," *The Christian Century* 93 (April 14, 1976): 363–64.

27. See one summary of the evidence, Mary K. Wakeman, *God's Battle with the Monster* (Leiden: E. J. Brill, 1973).

28. See Eberhard Jungel, who characterizes life as "relatedness" and death as "unrelatedness" (*Death: The Riddle and the Mystery* [Philadelphia: Fortress, 1974]).

29. Paul Hanson has situated such explorations in a context of world-weariness (*The Dawn of Apocalyptic* [Philadelphia: Fortress, 1975]).

30. See my comments in "From Hurt to Joy, from Death to Life."

31. Martin Hengel has articulated the crisis of Judaism in the Hellenistic period as the survival of the *ethnos* against the leveling, dehistoricizing claims of the polis (*Judaism and Hellenism* [Philadelphia: Fortress, 1974], 74 and passim). While the church must never become an *ethnos*, it is time for a reasserting of the claims of historical specificity against the polis if the vision of liberation is to endure with power.

CHAPTER 9: THE COSTLY LOSS OF LAMENT

1. Claus Westermann, *Praise and Lament in the Psalms* (Atlanta: John Knox, 1981), and also *The Psalms: Structure, Content and Message* (Minneapolis: Augsburg, 1980).

2. On the contributions of Hermann Gunkel and Sigmund Mowinckel, see A. R. Johnson, "The Psalms," in *The Old Testament and Modern Study*, ed. H. H. Rowley (Oxford: Clarendon Press, 1951), 162–209; John H. Hayes, *An Introduction to Old Testament Study* (Nashville: Abingdon, 1979), 285–317; and Ronald E. Clements, *One Hundred Years of Old Testament Interpretation* (Philadelphia: Westminster, 1976), 76–98.

3. Westermann, *Praise and Lament*, 33, 75, and passim.

4. How that intervention of God happened is unclear. The most formidable hypothesis is that of Hans Joachim Begrich, "Das Priesterliche Tora," *Zeitschrift für die alttestamentliche Wissenschaft* 66 (1936): 81–92. Begrich proposed that a

priestly oracle of salvation was spoken in the midst of the lament, which moved the speech from plea to praise. On Begrich's contribution, see Thomas M. Raitt, *A Theology of Exile* (Philadelphia: Fortress, 1977).

5. Westermann, *Praise and Lament*, 27–30.

6. Harvey H. Guthrie, *Theology as Thanksgiving* (New York: Seabury, 1981), 1–30, in my judgment, has a better understanding of thanksgiving as a vital form of response to God.

7. Guthrie, *Theology as Thanksgiving*, 18–19, shrewdly correlates form-critical insights with sociological realities. In contrast to Westermann, Guthrie regards thanksgiving as a more primal mode of faith than is praise. I am inclined to agree.

8. More recently form-critical scholarship has moved away from a rigid and one-dimensional notion of setting in life (*Sitz im Leben*) to a much more comprehensive and dynamic notion that would be, I suspect, more congenial to Westermann. On this development, see Rolf Knierim, "Old Testament Form Criticism Reconsidered," *Interpretation* 27 (1973): 435–68; and Martin J. Buss, "The Idea of Sitz im Leben—History and Critique," *Zeitschrift für die alttestamentliche Wissenschaft* 90 (1978): 157–70.

9. The relinquishment here accomplished is liturgical, rhetorical, and emotional, but I think it is important to correlate that form of relinquishment to the economic relinquishment urged by Marie Augusta Neale, *A Socio-Theology of Letting Go* (New York: Paulist, 1975). I believe these two forms of relinquishment are intimately related. It follows then that the loss of lament as a mode of letting go makes the possibility of economic relinquishment more problematic and sure to meet resistance.

10. See chap. 2 above, and Sigmund Mowinckel, *Psalmenstudien II, Das Thronbesteigungsfest Jahwäs und der Ursprung der Eschatologie* (Amsterdam: P. Schipper, 1961); Aubrey Johnson, *Sacral Kingship in Ancient Israel* (Cardiff: University of Wales Press, 1967). Various critiques are summarized in the presentations of Hayes and Clements.

11. Hans Schmidt, *Das Gebet der Angeklagten im Alten Testament*, Beihefte zur Zeitschrift für die alttestamentliche Wissenschaft 49 (Giessen: A. Töpelmann, 1928); Lienhard Delekat, *Asylie und Schutzorakel am Zionheiligtum* (Leiden: E. J. Brill, 1967); W. Beyerlin, *Die Rettung der Bedrängten in den Feindpsalmen der Einzelnen auf institutionelle Zusammenhänge untersucht*, Forschungen zur Religion und Literatur des Alten und Neuen Testaments 99 (Göttingen: Vandenhoeck & Ruprecht, 1970).

12. On the reality of social practice related to this psalm, see my paper, "Psalm 109: Three Times 'Steadfast Love,'" *Word and World* 5 (1985): 144–54.

13. Mowinckel's view was articulated in *Psalmenstudien*. It is summarized in *The Psalms in Israel's Worship* (Nashville: Abingdon, 1962), 2:4–8.

14. Rainer Albertz, *Persönliche Frömmigkeit und offizielle Religion*, Calwer Theologische Monographien 9 (Stuttgart: Calwer, 1978); Erhard Gerstenberger, *Der bittende Mensch: Bittritual und Klagelied des Einzelnen im Alten Testament*,

Wissenschaftliche Monographien zum Alten und Neuen Testament 51 (Neukirchen-Vluyn: Neukirchener Verlag, 1980).

15. For this understanding of the social power of speech forms, see Peter Berger and Thomas Luckmann, *The Social Construction of Reality* (Garden City, NY: Doubleday & Co., 1966). For this understanding applied specifically to the lament psalms, see chap. 8 above.

16 A convenient summary of the theory is offered by Charles V. Gerkin, *The Living Human Document* (Nashville: Abingdon, 1984), 82–96. I am grateful to Gerkin for suggesting some lines of my present research. Literature on the theory includes Otto Kernberg, *Object Relations Theory and Clinical Psychoanalysis* (New York: Jason Aronson, 1976); Kernberg, *Internal World and External Reality* (New York: Jason Aronson, 1981); Kernberg, *Object Relation Theory and Its Applications* (New York: Jason Aronson, 1981); Heinz Kohut, *The Analysis of the Self* (New York: International Universities Press, 1971); D. W. Winnicott, *The Maturational Processes and the Facilitating Environment: Studies in the Theory of Emotional Development* (Madison, WI: International Universities Press, 1965); and Harry Guntrip, *Psychoanalytic Theory, Therapy and the Self* (New York: Basic Books, 1971).

17. Winnicott, *Maturational Processes*, 145.

18. Winnicott, *Maturational Processes*, 145.

19. John Calvin, *Institutes of the Christian Religion*, ed. John T. McNeill, Library of Christian Classics 20 (Philadelphia: Westminster, 1960), 35–39, understands so shrewdly how the knowledge of God and the human creatures are interrelated. On Calvin's attempt to assert the utter sovereignty of God and God's propensity for relatedness, see Ford Lewis Battles, "God Was Accommodating Himself to Human Capacity," *Interpretation* (1977): 19–38.

20. On the social dimensions of the problem of evil and theodicy, see especially Jon Gunnemann, *The Moral Meaning of Revolution* (New Haven, CT: Yale University Press, 1979).

21. On the relation of God and justice in the Old Testament's understanding of theodicy, see my "Theodicy in a Social Dimension," *Journal for the Study of the Old Testament* 10, no. 33 (1985): 3–25, and *The Message of the Psalms* (Minneapolis: Augsburg, 1984), 168–76.

22. Cf. Claus Westermann, *The Structure of the Book of Job* (Philadelphia: Fortress, 1981), which claims that the poem of Job largely consists of these charges filed with the rather inappropriate refutations on the part of the friends.

23. On such boldness in biblical prayer, see Moshe Greenberg, *Biblical Prose Prayer* (Berkeley: University of California Press, 1983), 11–14 and passim.

24. On the daring attempt to make an appeal other than to God, see Job 19:25. Samuel Terrien, *Job: Poet of Existence* (Indianapolis: Bobbs-Merrill, 1957), 151, exposits such a reading of the text. This adventuresome thought is beyond the characteristic notion in the Old Testament that appeal can only be made once again to the same God. It is remarkable that Israel's rage against God did not drive Israel

away from God to atheism or idolatry, but more passionately into prayer addressed to God.

25. On the cruciality of this cry for the shape of Israel's faith, see James Plastaras, *The God of Exodus* (Milwaukee: Bruce Publishing Co., 1966), 49–59.

26. Paul D. Hanson, "The Theological Significance of Contradiction within the Book of Covenant," in *Canon and Authority*, ed. George W. Coats and Burke O. Long (Philadelphia: Fortress, 1977), 110–31. On the dialectic of compassion in response to human need, see Hanson, "War and Peace in the Hebrew Bible," *Interpretation* 38 (1984): 341–79.

27. This emphasis on social evil is a departure from the otherwise splendid statement of James L. Crenshaw, *Theodicy in the Old Testament* (Philadelphia: Fortress, 1983), 1–16. Crenshaw characterizes the issue only with reference to "moral, natural and religious" evil. I believe such a characterization is inadequate because of the great stress in the Old Testament on social justice and injustice.

28. Fascination with "meaning" was especially advanced by Paul Tillich, *Courage to Be* (New Haven, CT: Yale University Press, 1952), 41–42 and passim. In retrospect, Tillich's triad of death, guilt, and meaningfulness, as it applies to the modern period, is uncritically idealistic. A more materialist sense of social reality could not settle so readily for the category of "meaning" as the modern agenda.

29. On the function of civility as a mode of social control, see John Murray Cuddihy, *The Ordeal of Civility: Freud, Marx, Lévi-Strauss, and the Jewish Struggle with Modernity* (New York: Basic Books, 1974), and Norbert Elias, *Power and Civility* (New York: Pantheon Books, 1982).

30. Winnicott, *Maturational Processes*, characteristically speaks of the "good-enough" mother. He does not present a model of a perfect mother, but one who intuitively responds to the initiatives of the child. Winnicott observes that mothers characteristically operate in this way.

31. A variety of writers, such as Abraham Heschel, Dorothee Sölle, Kamo Kitamori, and Jürgen Moltmann, have now identified pathos as the mark of God that reshapes God's omnipotence. Elsewhere, I have suggested that the tension between God's omnipotence and God's pathos may be the shaping problem for doing Old Testament theology. See Walter Brueggemann, "A Shape for Old Testament Theology, I: Structure Legitimation," *Catholic Biblical Quarterly* 47 (1985): 28–46, and "A Shape for Old Testament Theology, II: Embrace of Pain," *Catholic Biblical Quarterly* 47 (1985): 395–415.

32. On the rhetorical power of the conjunction, see James Muilenburg, "The Form of Structure of the Covenantal Formulations," *Vetus Testamentum* 9 (1959): 74–79.

33. Robert Alter also has seen that the movement of silence and speech is crucial in this psalm: "On the contrary, the ancient Hebrew literary imagination reverts again and again to a bedrock assumption about the efficacy of speech, cosmogonically demonstrated by the Lord (in Genesis 1) who is emulated by man. In our poem, the speaker's final plea that God hear his cry presupposes the efficacy of speech, the truth-telling power with which language has been used to expose the supplicant's

plight. . . . The first two lines present a clear development of intensification of the theme of silence—from a resolution not to offend by speech, to muzzling the mouth, to preserving (in a chain of three consecutive synonyms) absolute muteness. The realized focal point of silence produces inward fire, a state of acute distress that compels a reversal of the initial resolution and issues in speech" (*The Art of Biblical Poetry* [New York: Basic Books, 1985], 67–73).

34. Erhard Gerstenberger, "Der klagende Mensch," in *Probleme biblischer Theologie*, ed. Hans Walter Wolff (Munich: Chr. Kaiser Verlag, 1971), 64–72, has shown how the complaint (in contrast to a lament of resignation) is in fact an act of hope.

35. Jose Miranda, *Communism in the Bible* (Maryknoll, NY: Orbis, 1981), 44, has concluded, "It can surely be said that the Psalter presents a struggle of the just against the unjust." His argument is an insistence that *rasha'* must not be rendered as a religious category, because it concerns issues of social power and social justice.

36. On the social situation of the *ger* ("sojourner"), see Frank Anthony Spina, "Israelites as *gerim*, 'Sojourners,' in Social and Historical Context," in *The Word of the Lord Shall Go Forth*, ed. Carol L. Meyers and M. O'Connor (Winona Lake, IL: Eisenbrauns, 1983), 321–35. Not unrelated to that social status, see Spina's more extended study on social rage, "The Concept of Social Rage in the Old Testament and the Ancient Near East" (PhD diss., University of Michigan, 1977). This psalm may be related to social rage around the question of theodicy.

CHAPTER 10: THE FEARFUL THIRST FOR DIALOGUE

1. George Steiner, *Real Presences* (Chicago: University of Chicago Press, 1989), 225.

2. See Walter Brueggemann, "Voice as Counter to Violence," *Calvin Theological Journal* 36, no. 1 (April 2001): 22–33.

3. On God's role in the daring dialogue of the book of Job, see Samuel E. Balentine, "'What Are Human Beings, That You Make So Much of Them?' Divine Disclosure from the Whirlwind: 'Look at Behemoth,'" in *God in the Fray: A Tribute to Walter Brueggemann*, ed. Tod Linafelt and Timothy K. Beal (Minneapolis: Fortress, 1998), 259–78.

4. See Susan A. Handelman, *The Slayers of Moses: The Emergence of Rabbinic Interpretation in Modern Literary Theory* (Albany: SUNY Press, 1982), and John Murray Cuddihy, *The Ordeal of Civility: Freud, Marx, Lévi-Strauss, and the Jewish Struggle with Modernity* (New York: Basic Books, 1974).

5. This is the same term from v. 21.

6. On the many voices of the self, see Roy Schafer, *Retelling a Life: Narration and Dialogue in Psychoanalysis* (New York: Basic Books, 1992), esp. chap. 2. It is clear that the recovery of "many voices" in current psychoanalytic theory and practice replicates what the Psalter knows and reflects.

7. The conditional construction is clear in the NRSV's use of "then" in each case, but it is not so clear or dramatic in Hebrew. I take the translation, however, to rightly reflect the force and intent of the rhetoric.

8. Claus Westermann, *The Praise of God in the Psalms* (Richmond, VA: John Knox, 1965), 25–30, has given classic formulation to the judgment that praise is a more faithful and noble act toward God than is thanks, and that thanks is a lesser and potentially more self-interested act. See the counteropinion of Harvey H. Guthrie Jr., *Theology as Thanksgiving: From Israel's Psalms to the Church's Eucharist* (New York: Seabury, 1981).

9. Fredrik Lindström, *Suffering and Sin: Interpretations of Illness in the Individual Complaint Psalms*, Coniectanea Biblica: Old Testament Series 37 (Stockholm: Almqvist & Wiksell International, 1994).

10. Ellen Davis, "Exploding the Limits: Form and Function in Psalm 22," *Journal for the Study of the Old Testament* 17, no. 53 (1992): 93–105.

CHAPTER 11: THE WONDER OF THANKS, SPECIFIC AND MATERIAL

1. See Walter Brueggemann, *From Whom No Secrets Are Hid: Introducing the Psalms*, ed. Brent A. Strawn (Louisville, KY: Westminster John Knox, 2014), 133–39.

CHAPTER 12: SPIRIT-LED IMAGINATION: REALITY PRACTICED IN A SUB-VERSION

1. On "miracle," see the stunning phrase of Martin Buber, *Moses: The Revelation and the Covenant* (Atlantic Highlands, NJ: Humanities Press International, 1988), 75, that miracle "can be defined at its starting point as an abiding astonishment."

2. Thanksgiving characteristically entailed both an utterance of gratitude and a material offering or, as we might say in Christian tradition, both "Word and sacrament." On the material offering, see Lev. 7:11–18 and Ps. 116:12–19. On the theology of such action, see Harvey H. Guthrie Jr., *Theology as Thanksgiving: From Israel's Psalms to the Church's Eucharist* (New York: Seabury, 1981).

3. See the discussion of I. John Hesselink, "Karl Barth on Prayer," in Karl Barth, *Prayer*, 50th anniversary ed., ed. Donald E. Saliers (Louisville, KY: Westminster John Knox, 2002), 75–84, and his references to Barth, *Church Dogmatics*, III/3.

4. Claus Westermann, *The Praise of God in the Psalms* (Richmond, VA: John Knox, 1965); see also Patrick D. Miller, *They Cried to the Lord: The Form and Theology of Biblical Prayer* (Minneapolis: Fortress, 1994), chap. 3.

5. See the exposition of "the cry" in Israel's faith by James L. Kugel, *The God of Old: Inside the Lost World of the Bible* (London: Free Press, 2003), chap. 5.

6. On the contemporary dominant version of reality and its capacity for self-maintenance, see Charles Reich, *Opposing the System* (New York: Crown, 1995).